OJIBWAY CEREMONIES

Basil Johnston

Illustrations by David Beyer

University of Nebraska Press
Lincoln and London

First Bison Book printing: 1990
Most recent printing indicated by the first digit below:
10   9   8   7   6   5   4

Library of Congress Cataloging-in-Publication Data
Johnston, Basil.
Ojibway ceremonies / Basil Johnston: illustrations by David Beyer.
—Bison book ed.
p. cm.
ISBN 0-8032-7573-0
1. Ojibwa Indians—Fiction. 2. Indians of North America—Canada
—Fiction. I. Title.
PR9199.3.J597035   1990
813'.54—dc20
89-24972 CIP

Reprinted by arrangement with McClelland and Stewart

Contents

Preface to the Bison Book Edition

The book *Ojibway Ceremonies* came about in the following way.

As guest editor of *Tawow,* a magazine devoted to Native issues and themes and published in Ottawa, Canada, I met Ernest Willey, a Kwakiutl Indian, then residing in Toronto, Ontario, while I was scouting for writers for my projected theme, Native World Views.

After hearing Mr. Willey speak on his tribe to an audience at the Canadian Indian Centre in Toronto in 1976, I asked him to write an article on some aspect of his tribe's culture and heritage. He declined, giving as his reason his inexperience in writing. However, he was willing to tell me about one tribal ceremony in which he took part as a principal and let me write the text.

Before Mr. Willey described the ceremony he explained that, though it was popularly known as the Cannibal Dance outside the Kwakiutl tribe, it had nothing to do with the eating of human flesh and that it was not a dance but an enactment that appeared like a dance to strangers. His tribe called it Hah-Mah-Tsa, an initiation.

Prior to the ceremony, the initiate was regarded in a formal sense as outside society but connected to it by virtue of his dependence upon it for his nourishment, guidance, and growth. Following the ceremony, the initiate was a full member of the Kwakiutl society, no longer a dependent or a recipient but a contributor and a benefactor. Only when a person could contribute as a chanter, dancer, hunter, and fisherman could he be admitted formally and actually into tribal society.

But physical abilities and skills in hunting, fishing, chanting, and dancing are not alone enough to qualify a person for admission into society. The initiate must understand himself and his relationship to the other members of the community and to society in general.

When the elders of the community deemed that a young person had reached the age of understanding and was ready to be inducted, they gave him and his parents notice of their intent to initiate him

1

into full membership in the society of the tribe through the performance of the Hah-Mah-Tsa. Invitations to attend the ceremony were also sent out to other communities.

Four days prior to the performance of the Hah-Mah-Tsa, guests began to arrive to take part in the preparation period. As each canoe arrived at the host village, the chiefs and elders welcomed and greeted guests with speeches and dances. The candidate was presented to each group.

That same evening Mr. Willey was conducted to a remote secluded area where he was to keep vigil for four days and three nights, during which time he was to seek a vision and to meditate on the awesome choice that he was about to make. The temporary banishment from family and community symbolized his state and condition and status, that of a nonmember, an outcast. For the next four days, until recalled, Ernest Willey meditated upon his being and life and the duties and obligations to his tribe that he had to undertake and fulfill after his symbolic rebirth into society.

In those four days he had to choose between selfishness and selflessness, between evil and good. If he chose the former, he had to remain outside the community and society, an outcast, an isolate; if he opted for the latter, he would be admitted into the society of men and women of good will. Whatever choice he was going to make would reflect the fundamental understanding of human nature that the elders of the tribe and his parents had instilled in him. According to some people, men and women were by nature evil; others believed in the innate goodness of humankind. But to the Kwakiutl, men and women were neither good nor evil; they only possessed a disposition for selfishness and selflessness, evil or good. Men and women were free to make choices between them. If a community was to thrive and prosper, it must be composed of men and women committed to good.

If the initiate was to choose selflessness, he must first overcome and repudiate what the tribe regarded as evil. In the eyes and in the judgment of the Kwakiutl, the worst forms of selfishness are the desire to dominate others, disregard of the needs of others, fear and cowardice (weakness), and surrender to carnal appetites. These four vices making up selfishness were construed as acts, not necessarily directed against the physical well-being of individuals or against society but against the moral code and spiritual fabric of the community. Before an initiate could espouse the good, he had to understand what was regarded as offensive to the community and to society; only then could he appreciate what he was repudiating.

To impress on youth the repugnance with which they should look on selfishness, the Kwakiutl dramatized it by comparing it to the act of eating human flesh, not just ordinary flesh, but the entrails of a corpse. Selfishness ate the soul-spirit of an individual just as it surely gnawed at the core of society.

By understanding the malignity of selfishness, the initiate would more freely and willingly renounce it and espouse the good—which was equated to harmony, order, and compliance with reason—within the self, and to respect kin and neighbors outside of the self. In order to achieve this state the initiate had to master his predilection for selfishness and his carnality. If a person could master the self, it was assumed that he could govern his urges to enlarge his place and encroach upon that of others through force or guile, that he could manage his impulses to put his own needs and comforts first to the detriment of others, and that he could regulate his instinct for self-preservation and risk his safety in order to deliver a neighbor from danger. If he could control himself, he could help spread and maintain harmony in the community.

Because men and women were part of a world that is larger than their villages or their tribes, they must live in harmony with the seasons, the mountains, valleys, and rivers; with bears, wolves, eagles, ravens, otters, whales, and salmon who have an equal right to life and tenure upon Mother Earth. That humankind be more clever than beasts with their needs met only by the animals in the forest or lake did not confer upon them a preeminence that supercedes the right of animals to *their* place and tenure on Mother Earth. Men and women are co-tenants with other creatures upon the land and must respect the rights and lives and tenure of the animals, birds, and fish, if *they* are to survive.

Once the initiate understood and accepted his place in society and in the world, he knew the purpose of life. It was this conception of man and his society that the Kwakiutl ritualized in the celebration of the Hah-Mah-Tsa.

On the fourth and last day of the fast and vigil, the sponsors came for Ernest Willey and escorted him back to the village.

There are four dances in the Hah-Mah-Tsa. In the first, the initiate petitions through chant and act the community and the tribe for admission into their society and promises to abide by the terms and conditions of membership.

Next is the dance and chant of renunciation of selfishness. At the commencement of this dance, the initiate is accompanied by four malevolent figures, the Grizzly Bear, the Thunderbird, the Killer Whale, and one other unnamed form representing the four aspects of selfishness. Midway during the performance of the dance of re-

3

nunciation, the mood and the tone and the pace change. The dance is transformed into one of triumph, triumph of spirit over flesh, good over evil. Ernest Willey formally declared his choice in chant. At that moment the four malevolent figures were transformed into benevolent, protective patrons whose function was to guide Ernest Willey along the road of selflessness and upright conduct.

The metamorphosis that takes place suggests that evil is external to man's nature and is visited upon man from without; by corollary, good is to be found and sought outside human nature. The Hah-Mah-Tsa symbolizes not so much a vanquishment of evil but a person's capacity to negate evil by transforming it into good.

At the conclusion of this dance of renunciation, the presiding elder conferred the name of Kah-Sha-La on Ernest Willey as a sign of admission and acceptance. Although the name was bestowed by the master of ceremonies, it represented the gift of all those present. The new name embodied the character of the initiate. From this day Ernest Willey was to bear the name with dignity and to comport himself in a manner worthy of the gift of the people. He had to uphold his name as he would his reputation, for it was nothing less than that.

After Ernest Willey had received his name, a woman conducted him into the circle for the final dance, which was to confirm his admission into society. It was only fitting that since a woman brought him into being it should be a woman who confirmed his membership into the community of men and women. Only a woman could make him complete and give him meaning.

When the ceremony was over the village gave a feast in Kah-Sha-La's honor. "I was proud," Mr. Willey recalled, "that I was now a full member of the tribe and society, that I was adjudged capable of contributing to my people. And yet I was uneasy, afraid that I might fail and not live up to the expectations of my people. You see the Hah-Mah-Tsa is not just a spectacle; it ritualizes many of our beliefs and understandings. Have you comparable ceremonies in your tribe?"

Though I knew some, I had to confess to Mr. Willey that I did not know them as well as I ought.

For the next two years before Mr. Willey returned to his tribe in British Columbia, he and I met several times to discuss and compare our respective tribal customs and ceremonies, but knowing little of my tribe's ceremonies except what I had read, I could not enlighten my friend. The upshot was that I resolved to learn more about my tribe's spiritual heritage and traditions to better prepare me to carry out my plan to write books about my tribe.

When I told Mr. Willey of my intention to learn more and to write

4

about my tribe's ceremonies, he advised me to reexamine whatever I had read and whatever I would read on the subject and to try to understand the ceremonies in terms of my tribe's beliefs, values, and language. "You must get to know your language even better than you now do," he suggested. To reinforce his advice, Mr. Willey repeated what he had previously told me: that though many tribal ceremonies appeared as dances to casual and uninformed observers and were described as such by most anthropologists, the performances were in reality dramas enacting and ritualizing beliefs, events, stories, and understandings. Mr. Howard Skye and his nephew James, both Onondagas of the Six Nations in Brantford, Ontario, and members of the Longhouse Society offered me similar advice.

Over the next two years I read as many books as I could lay my hands on: *The Indians of Canada* by John McLean, *The First Americans* by Daniel Jacobson, *Indians of North America* by Harold Driver, *Patterns of Culture* by Ruth Benedict, *Indians of the Americas*, a publication of the National Geographic Society, *The Sacred Pipe* by Joseph E. Brown, *Indians of the Americas* by Edwin R. Embree, *The American Heritage Book of Indians* by William Brandon, *The Canadian Indian* by Fraser Symington, *Red Man's Religion* by Ruth Underhill, *Chippewa Customs* by Frances Densmore, *Ojibwa Texts* by William Jones (in both the English and Ojibwa texts), *Traditional History of the Ojibway Nation* by George Copway, *Hiawatha* by Henry Wadsworth Longfellow, *The Indian Heritage of America* by Alvin Josephy, Jr., and many, many others.

Although the texts yielded physical description aplenty in volumes and in driblets, none delivered that tone, those meanings that I was looking for.

In the fall of 1978 I met Mr. Sam Ozawamik (Brown Beaver) of Wikwemikong, Manitoulin Island, at Couchiching, Ontario, where I had been invited to tell tribal stories. At the end of one evening session Mr. Ozawamik introduced himself and remarked, "You seem to know where the tribal stories fit in their relationship to another. I know many stories but I'm not sure where they belong. I can teach you if you want to learn."

No offer for guidance could have come at a more propitious time and I readily accepted Sam Ozawamik's offer.

Between the autumn of 1978 and that of 1981, during the writing of the drafts of the text of *Ojibway Ceremonies,* I frequently called Sam for the meaning of words and the meaning of ceremonies and rituals. Up to this time, though I spoke the tribal language, I had taken it for granted. Under Sam's tutelage I came to realize the richness, beauty, and depth of the words and the language.

What I learned was that the words in our tribal language had meanings more fundamental than the primary ones that were commonly and readily understood. To know this character of words is crucial in understanding how the tribe perceived and expressed what they saw, heard, felt, tasted, and smelled in the world and what they thought and how they felt about the world of ideas.

Everyone knew the primary meaning of words. There was not a person who did not know that the word "Anishnabeg" referred to a member of his tribe, though few knew that it meant in its most fundamental sense, "people of good intentions." But it meant more than that; it reflected how men and women saw themselves influencing their notions and their exercise of equality, as well as governing their communion with the manitous and Kitchi-Manitou.

And because they could not or dared not define God or the deities, or explain or reduce to human terms certain phenomena, they invented the word *manitou*, which at times, depending upon context, might mean spirit, but which in its more fundamental senses meant talent, attributes, potencies, potential, substance, essence, and mystery.

If one is to know what a medicine man or woman is doing by addressing plants and offering tobacco as he or she gathers and prepares medicines, or to whom the celebrant is offering the incense of tobacco in the smoking of the Sacred Pipe, it is essential to know precisely the sense in which the term *manitou* is being used. Otherwise one may be led, as many have been, into thinking that the Ojibway were chanting and performing rituals to great and little spirits. For me it was absolutely essential that I know the distinctions before I set out to record my tribe's ceremonies.

There were many other matters that I had to learn before I began, such as the mythological origins of rituals, customs, and ceremonies.

I dedicate this work to the memory of my father and mother, Rufus and Mary, who gave me the advantage of my tribe's language. I also wish to acknowledge the guidance of my friend and teacher Sam Ozawamik, and the encouragement of my friend and colleague, Dr. E. S. Rogers, now deceased, formerly of the Department of Ethnology of the Royal Ontario Museum. I wish, too, to express my appreciation to my own family and friends for their patience during the long, silent work.

Preface

To understand the origin and the nature of life, existence, and death, the Ojibway speaking peoples conducted inquiries within the soul-spirit that was the very depth of their being. Through dream or vision quest they elicited revelation – knowledge that they then commemorated and perpetuated in story and re-enacted in ritual. But in addition to insight, they also gained a reverence for the mystery of life which animated all things: human-kind, animal-kind, plant-kind, and the very earth itself.

In private, hunters and fishermen sought the patronage and the pardon of the manitous (mysteries) who presided over the animals and the birds; and medicine men and women invoked the mysteries to confer curative powers upon the herbs that were used in their preparations. In public, the people conducted rituals and ceremonies to foster upright living; petitioned Kitche Manitou and the deities for blessing; or offered thanksgiving for game and abundant harvest. From the origin and form of these ceremonies, and from the substance of the chants and prayers, the Ojibway speaking peoples' understanding and interpretation of moral order can be discovered.

I dedicate this work to the memory of my father and mother, Rufus and Mary, both deceased. I also wish to acknowledge the guidance of my friend and teacher, Sam Zawamik, and the encouragement of my friend and colleague, Dr. E.S. Rogers of the Department of Ethnology of the Royal Ontario Museum. I wish, too, to express my appreciation to my own family and friends for their patience during the long, silent work.

List of Place Names

LAC DU FLAMBEAU / *Wausswaugunning* (Place of Torch
    Fishing)

LAKE MICHIGAN / *Mishigameeng* (Big Lake)

LAKE ST. CLAIR / *Wauwi-Autinoong* (Round Lake)

LAKE SUPERIOR / *Kitche-Ojibway-Gameeng* (Great Sea of
    the Anishnabeg)

MADELEINE ISLAND / *Moningwunaekauning* (Place of
    the Yellow Woodpecker)

MICHILIMACKINAC / *Mishi Mackinakong* (Place of the
    Great Turtle)

NIAGARA FALLS / *Kitche-Gaugeedjwung* (Great Edge-
    Over)

NIPIGON / *Nipigong* (Place of Waters)

NIPISSING / *Nipissing* (Place of the Elms)

SAULT STE. MARIE / *Boweting* (Place of Rapids)

THUNDER BAY / *Gaumeenautikawayauk* (Place of Many
    Berries)

TIMAGAMI / *Teemigameeng* (Deep Lake)

The Naming Ceremony

Wauweendaussowin

THE BEGINNING

Waubizeequae (Swan Woman) cradled her baby in the crook of her arm, and pressed it to her breast.

"Ogauh! Would you ask Cheengwun to name our son?" she asked her husband.

Ogauh (Pickerel) hesitated. "Should we not wait until he is a little bigger, a little older?" he said. He was not against the naming of their son, he simply felt no urgency for doing so. Among the Anishnabeg (or Ojibway) people, haste was unnecessary. Babies were often named much later, a year or sometimes two years after they were born. For people to be named after they were ten or even twelve was not unknown.

But Waubizeequae insisted. "I will not wait until our baby is sick before we have him named. I wish to have him named soon."

Ogauh nodded and got to his feet. He crossed the village grounds which were vibrant with the laughter of children and vital with the stir of men and women in their tasks. Children either played tag or wrestled or carried bundles of twigs and branches for the fires. Near the centre of the village, an old woman sat on the ground bent over a hide that she was fashioning into a jacket. Further on, Auniquot (Cloud) was lashing ribs to the gunwale of a canoe; and beyond that, women were hanging strips of meat on horizontal poles or pressing berries in birch bark containers. Except for the running of the children, there was no attempt to hurry the pace of

13

life. Even the sounds of the village, the barking of the ever-present dogs, the quiet talk of women, and the muffled laughter of old men, seemed relaxed.

Cheengwun (Meteor) was not at home. Kitchi-Zaudee (Great Poplar) thought that the old man had gone up the hill to gather medicine at the far end of the ridge. When Ogauh finally found Cheengwun he was on his knees in the middle of his work, and because gathering medicine was much more than an act of digging roots, he did not disturb the medicine man. Chopping leaves and pruning stalks and unearthing roots was in itself an enactment of ritual, the deepest expression of reverence for the mystery of life and the essence and curative power of the plant. During the collection, Cheengwun addressed the plants as sentient beings, petitioning them to confer their healing powers upon the sick, and asking their pardon for removing them from the land and from their hold upon life. "The sick need you. You are strong and well and have done your work. Kitche Manitou has endowed you with an essence for your good and for the well-being of others. I have come for you, not for myself, but for the sick ... that they may get well. Pardon me for taking you. To you and Kitche Manitou I offer this tobacco." Thus Cheengwun spoke to each plant as he removed it from its place and implanted an offering of tobacco in the soil.*

Cheengwun folded and tied his bundle before he got up. "There must be something," he said, without looking up, as if he knew that Ogauh had been there all along.

Ogauh spoke. "I have come to ask you to name our son."

"Oh!" Cheengwun aspirated an expression which by its tone was intended to give consent, before he swung the bundle over his right shoulder.

On the way back to the village Ogauh walked behind Cheengwun, who stopped several times to examine plants by feeling their texture, handling them lightly as one would touch a delicate and sensitive object. His mind and eye were focussed on nothing but the plants that grew in profusion on the forest floor. It was as if Ogauh was not there. Only the plants mattered.

But back in the village, just as they parted, Cheengwun said to Ogauh, "I will let you know the time."

THE SEARCH

On the surface, giving a name was easy. But before the ceremony could take place there were days of meditation and nights of dreaming. For a name was not merely an appellation, or a term of address; it was an identity at the time it was bestowed, merging later into reputation. Until named, a child was without identity except to its mother and father. It was no more than a presence with a potential and, with care and good fortune, a future. That and nothing more. Hence the namer's task was not a light matter. Not only did the namer have to give a name, but he had also, by virtue of being a namer, to assume certain responsibilities for the child. By being asked to name a child, the namer was asked to be like a second father.

Even though old Cheengwun had named many members of the tribe, he never found it easy. He had to go beyond memory and into the realm of dream for enlightenment, or perhaps revelation. That was the most difficult of all. Sometimes a name came soon after he began his quest for dreams. More often, months of meditation passed before the patrons of dreams took Cheengwun into their world and gave him revelation. This time it took Cheengwun two months.

When finally the event occurred, he went to Ogauh's lodge to announce the day of the naming. "In four days time," he said, "I will name your child."

PREPARATION

During the next four days Cheengwun's wife cleaned the lodge, replacing the floor covering with fresh cedar boughs and re-arranging the household bundles. Their godson must breathe in the sweet scent of cedar and look upon order and cleanliness. Perhaps the child would somehow absorb a sense of beauty and harmony. But the real reason for the renewal of the lodge was to render it fitting for the most important event in a person's life: the receiving of an identity through ceremony and name. From then on the child would bear a name and have a place near the tribal fire and in tribal thoughts. The name that the child would bear was a gift of the spirits, bestowed through ritual by a namer; a gift to be cherished by the named and respected for its origin within the tribe. For such a solemn and sacred occasion, the place of naming was to be clean.

And Cheengwun's wife prepared a feast for the guests, the grandparents and the parents of the infant. There was to be venison and wild turkey and smoked whitefish; cranberries, apples, blueberries, and maple syrup.

On the evening of the fourth day, the guests arrived. Ogauh and his parents and his wife's parents brought gifts of tobacco, corn, gauntlets, and leggings. Ogauh presented Cheengwun with a pipe that he had made especially for the occasion. After they had talked for a while, Cheengwun said, "Ahow!" and he motioned to Waubizeequae, the mother of the child, to sit near him.

"First, let me tell you how I was enabled to give names ...."

CHEENGWUN'S GIFT

I received the gift in dream, a long time ago. I did not seek it. It was given freely during sleep. I was taken from this world and transported through the skies, past the nearest stars and beyond the farthest, to another world. I was set down at an entrance where an old woman greeted me and warned that should I sleep within sleep or eat food during my visit, I would die. Then she told me that I was free to wander wherever I pleased. And so I roamed this strange land.

With its mountains and valleys, plains and forests, lakes and rivers, the land seemed very much like our own. But the colours were different. Never had I seen colours as bright. I do not know whether they were in themselves more brilliant than any I had ever seen, or whether my senses were more keen. And the land's sounds were wonderful. No birdsong on earth could compare to the songs of the birds that echoed in those forests. No thunder on earth could have been as loud as the thunder there. And yet even the most awesome winds in this land were as balmy as our south winds.

I went from place to place without seeing anyone, although I passed many deserted villages. In these villages the lodges were empty, and the food racks had been stripped by birds and animals. Fireplaces were cold, and tools scattered. There was no one, not even dogs, and I found this strange.

I continued on my way, certain that I would eventually come upon people somewhere. Perhaps, I thought, they were at some festival. Then, while I was making my way down the slope of a hill, I heard voices below – the voices of children yelling. I went down the hill as quietly as I could, until I could see the children between the trees; and then, because I did not want to startle them, and because I was uneasy about my own safety, I crept forward on my knees until I reached a grove of cedars that concealed me from view.

There were fifteen boys and girls, their faces black with charcoal, their hair matted and unkempt, running on the surface of a lake. Back and forth, from end to end they ran, with sweat streaming down their faces and spines, strength ebbing from their legs. Only will sustained them, and even this would soon not be enough. How long they had been running I did not know. But from the way that their shoulders sagged and their knees buckled I could guess that it had been a long time. At last, one by one they collapsed on the bank, where they lay heaving and gasping for breath.

After a while some of the runners sat up with a look of lingering pain on their faces. I could not take my eyes from them. I had never seen such sadness. First, there was the pain of tortured bone and muscle that subsides only with rest. But keener and more abiding than the pain of body was the pain of soul that dulled the eyes of the runners. They had not fully rested when a voice to my right urged them back. "You have had your rest! You must run a little longer before you can go home."

I crept forward to see who was in charge of the runners. It was an old woman; and she, too, suffered from pain that was soul deep. Only late in the afternoon did she call the runners from the lake.

There was something about that lake and its waters that drew me. Boys and girls had run and walked upon its surface without sinking; and yet I knew, from its motion, that it was not ice. At the water's edge I immersed my hand, and then my arm. Then I took off my moccasins and leggings and waded out until I was thigh deep. I could not understand it. Why was

17

it that the water did not bear me up as it did the children?

While I was standing in the water I felt a change come over me – as if I were being compressed. The next moment I was at the bottom of the lake, swimming and gliding about easily. For the first time I saw the bed of a lake. It was no longer a mystery.

All night I swam, looking under ledges, wiggling through weeds and reeds, meeting trout and whitefish and bass and perch. How still and clear it was within the depths! I looked up at the moving surface, and beyond that into the height of the skies. Through the moving glass of the surface I saw the moon and stars and clouds distorted as if in a dream. When day came, the light added yet another dimension to my sight.

Shortly after daybreak, the children came and began to run. From the bottom I could see their warped and curved forms flashing by and hear their muffled cries. The echoes of their footsteps pitched from bank to shoal and re-echoed, like the sound of cracking ice passing somewhere in infinity. While I was held by the images and the echoes and the ripple of the echoes, I was suddenly seized and brought to the surface of the lake. "Grandmother! Grandmother!" shouted my captors. "Look what we found." Taking me by the hand (I was no longer a water creature, but man once more, transformed by some process at the instant of emergence), they led me to the shore and ushered me to the old woman.

She waved her hand to the children who had crowded around. "Keep running!" she ordered. And the children returned to their exercises.

"Why do you make them run?" I asked. "They are not beasts. Can you not see that they are tired?"

In a voice full of sadness, the old woman spoke. "A long time ago, a man challenged the Weendigoes to a contest. Had he won the race, he would have killed the Weendigoes; but the Weendigoes won, and the tribe paid a terrible price. A Weendigo came to the villages every day to kill someone, and they made a sport and a mockery of our suffering. They promised to stop killing the tribe should any man or woman ever defeat them in a race. It was a terrible thing for that man, long ago, to have challenged the spirits ...." The old woman sighed. "There is no hope. Still we run. And we will run until we are

18

no more. Once there were thousands ... many villages. Now there are only fifteen; tomorrow fourteen; and the next day, thirteen ... Soon it will be over, but until then we must go through the ritual of fast and quest for dream. We will petition our patrons and our guardians for relief, and we will run .... I will be the last."

And the children ran until they fell into helpless heaps. Only then did the old woman call them to go home. Throughout the entire journey, they asked who I was and where I had come from; and I answered them as best I could. When we reached the village, the children rested while the old woman picked mushrooms that grew in great abundance. She fed each of the children one small mushroom, and even though the children were hungry and begged for more she would not allow them another one. Not until they had defeated the Weendigoes would they get more than one; and then, there would be a feast. She offered me a dish of mushrooms, the food of the dead, but in spite of my hunger I refused. After the children ate their meal and drank a little water, the old woman bade them sleep and seek dream.

I felt drowsy, but I dared not sleep. To stay awake I watched the stars – and the clouds that curled and writhed across the skies, never keeping to one form or shape. The more distant clouds moved slowly, as if their mass held them back. The nearer clouds coursed across the face of the night sky, dark wisps and balls ever-changing and swift. Flashing ahead, the lead cloud murmured: *I leave you behind. You are too slow. I leave you behind.*

In the morning the old woman came to my shelter to offer a meal of mushrooms. I dared not touch them; but when she asked me what I had dreamed, I told her. She fed the children one mushroom each, and gave each a drink of water, asking them also what they had dreamed. Most of them shook their heads. Those who had dreamed recounted their dreams. Then, even before the children had finished their meagre ration, the earth rumbled and a shadow shrouded the village. A voice like thunder rolled. "It is time," it shouted. "Hurry! I cannot wait." The children blackened their faces and left without a word.

I got up to go, but the old woman held me back. She blackened her face and got on her knees and rocked slowly back and forth, wailing and keening. Later that morning the children straggled back to camp, wretched in despair and defeat. There were fourteen. Their champion had been overcome and borne away.

Afterwards, the children came to me. They crowded around me and took my hand as if my touch and presence would lend them strength and comfort in the final days of their existence. They asked me again and again how long I was going to remain with them. When I told them that I did not know, they begged me as their "grandfather" to stay.

I then asked them what their names were, what their totems were, where they came from, who they were, and if any of them were brothers or sisters. They shook their heads. They were strangers to themselves and to one another. They had been brought together by the old woman from various parts of the country to conceal them from the Weendigoes, and although they called her "grandmother" even she did not know who they were. They were strangers, nameless .... To cheer them, I told stories the entire day, and by evening some of the children were smiling. They asked me to sleep by their side.

But I did not sleep. For the first part of the night I sat watching the shadows of trees, listening to their leaves rustle and ripple as if an invisible hand were combing them, or a spirit were gliding through their crowns. Sometimes the trees would groan and crack, as if a great burden were pressed upon their spines. My vision and my hearing were upon nearby things; my mind was upon the children and their fate. Suddenly, I heard a small, triumphant cry: *I leave you behind. You are too slow. I leave you behind.* I looked down to see where the voice came from, and saw a colony of ants moving towards a patch of tall grasses. A young ant was outrunning his companions. As I watched, the ants swarmed and vanished, and the voice and the words passed out of my hearing.

During the morning meal, a voice again rumbled across the skies. "It is time. Hurry! I cannot wait." The children looked at me in terror. "Grandfather, come with us!" they pleaded.

From the camp to the lake no word was spoken. There was no wind, there was no song of bird to lift the awful silence of that last and final walk. At the shore, the children broke away and hid in bushes, ravines, behind rocks—wherever they could find concealment.

"You cannot hide!" sounded the voice. "I will find you and I will take you all!"

I went out onto the open lake, and stood upon the water without sinking.

"Who are you?" the giant demanded, when he saw me.

"I am Cheengwun."

"Come then, and race. Hurry! I cannot wait."

"I will leave you behind," I said.

"How dare you believe that you can match or surpass me!" bellowed the giant. "You! Little man! How can you believe that?" And he laughed, sneering.

"I dreamed that I would leave you behind."

"Ha!" he spat out. "A dream? No one has ever beaten me or my brothers. Your powers can never match my powers. Your dreams are nothing compared to my dreams. I have fasted for ten days, and I dreamed that my challenger was a snail who did not go the length of my footstep before I had arrived at the finish line. Around my neck I wear this snail as a symbol of my speed and triumph. Look, little man! Where is your emblem?"

"I do not wear one. My dream is my power."

"Do you know the stake?"

"Yes."

"And you still want to run against me?"

"Yes. I will leave you behind."

And we ran, from one end of the lake to the other. I ran easily, taking the lead from the start. At the finish line I waited for the Weendigo, whose eyes were bright and large with terror. He sat down at my feet pleading for mercy, pledging nevermore to return. But I did not trust the monster. I took my club and killed him.

I returned to the shore and called the children from their hiding places. They seemed uneasy. I told them that I had outrun the Weendigo and had slain him. To remove their doubts, I led the children and the old woman to the far end of the lake to show them the corpse of the dead Weendigo.

They all shrank back from the body in horror. I thought

they would be glad, but their terror seemed even greater than before. The old woman explained that there were many Weendigoes, and that the others would come to avenge the death of their brother – perhaps that afternoon.

But no one came; and by evening the children were smiling. Even the old woman relented, and allowed the children as many mushrooms as they could eat. It was a feast, a celebration, and for a little while they forgot their troubles. But when it was time to sleep, the old fears returned. "Grandfather," they asked, "are you going to run against the Weendigoes tomorrow?"

"Yes. If they come."

"Are you not afraid? There are many!"

"No," I answered. And that was the truth. I felt no fear. I had my dream.

At daybreak, the ground trembled, and a voice shattered the stillness of the dawn. "Cheengwun! I have come for you! You slew my brother, and for that I will kill you. Are you ready?"

"I am ready!" I shouted back.

As I left the camp the children whispered, "Grandfather, be careful. Leave him behind."

At the shore waited the Weendigo, hate in his eyes, hate in his presence, and death in his breath. But I was not afraid. I stood a little way from the monster, not because I feared him, but because I did not trust him. When we ran, I did not need to exert myself, for my opponent was slow. I stayed ahead of him, looking back from time to time, and I could see terror in his eyes and on his mouth. At the opposite end of the lake I waited for him. He fell to the ground exhausted, and began to cower and to plead for his life, promising that his tribe would never again prey upon people. But I clubbed him, as I had clubbed his brother.

Then I went in search of the other Weendigoes who lived in the country. I slew them all, except some who fled to the north. When I returned to the village of the children they were in mourning, wailing, their faces blackened for my death; but when they learned what I had done, their mourning changed to celebration.

That night the children feasted and laughed, chanted and

danced. During the festival, the old woman reminded me that the children did not have names. It had not mattered before, because they had been destined to die – but now that they were going to live it would be a good thing to have names. The old woman asked me to do this. I had safeguarded the lives of the children, and now I could confer upon each of them an identity. She would help them fulfil their potential.

At the end of their festival I called the children to me and told them what I was about to do. Their eyes lit up. They had adopted me as their grandfather; now, by act of naming, I was adopting them as my grandchildren. I told them that the names I was going to bestow upon them were gifts, and that they were to cherish the names and never defile the gift.

Beginning with the eldest, I conferred on each child a name corresponding to some characteristic that I had observed. And I remember the names: Animkee-Waewidum (Speaks Thunder); Meegwun-Geezhigoquae (Plume Sky Woman); Makatae-Geezis (Black Sky); Mino-Nodiniquae (Gentle Wind Woman); Shkotae-Auniquot (Fire Cloud); Zaugutauhquae (Little Bud Woman); Pigook (Arrow); Zhaegwaukomaun (Dull Knife); Ogidaubik (At the Summit); Bookidoohnsh (Pear); Tibik-Inossae (Night Walker); Pugumaugun (War Club); Kitugaukoohnse (Fawn); and Gazhee-Aush (Swift Flight).

After relating the tale of his gift, Cheengwun paused for a moment. Then he addressed the infant in the cradle-board. "N'Kweemiss," he said, a term that meant godson or even namesake. "N'Kweemiss, I have had a good dream. You will have a good name. Listen, and I will tell you my dream." He placed a small bow and arrow by the baby, his gift to his grandson by the ritual of naming. His voice became gentler and lower. "Listen to my dream," he said, turning to Waubizeequae and Ogauh. "Tell it to your son often. It is a powerful dream, full of good medicine."

THE STORY OF THE NAME

An old man lived alone with his grandson on the bank of a river in a remote part of the country. They had fled there to hide from giants who were killing the tribe. Only the old man and his grandson had survived.

As soon as the little boy was old enough, the grandfather sent him out to hunt. The first time he was on the trail, the boy was startled by a creature who spun out of a thicket. Frightened, the boy ran back to his grandfather to whom he described the frightful creature. The grandfather explained that the animal was a rabbit, harmless and good for eating. The boy went back and killed the rabbit. As it was the boy's first kill, the grandfather cooked the rabbit and conducted the First Kill Ceremony. The boy was now a hunter, able to look after himself and his grandfather. Never again did he fear anything or anyone. He grew more skilful with bow and arrow and became bolder in his hunting trips.

On one of his hunting expeditions the young man came upon an abandoned camp site. The framework of the lodge was warped and bent and very frail; nearby was a small circle of stones for a fireplace. Someone had struck a camp and a fire. Someone had come, lingered, and gone on.

But although they had gone, the suggestion of a presence had been left behind. There was no other sign. All prints between past and present had been washed away by rain, snow, and wind. But the presence remained – and the thought that there were other beings both disturbed and excited the young man. There were other people, besides himself and his grandfather!

He ran home and told his grandfather of the abandoned camp site. But the old man shook his head. "It cannot be," he said. "It cannot be. We are the only ones alive; all the rest were killed. It cannot be." The old man then recounted how a man had once entered into a wager with the giants and had lost. He told his grandson how the giants had punished the tribe by killing every man, woman, and child. "I hid. I hid you. There are no other survivors. You must be mistaken. You must forget this false thing you have thought."

But the grandson returned to the abandoned encampment the next day. As he stood near the framework of the lodge, he heard a voice addressing him. The voice seemed to come from some point in the past, spoken by someone just beyond vision.

"I am your patron," said the voice. "I have chosen you to avenge the sufferings inflicted by the giants upon your people – and to you will I give the means to overcome your oppressors. When you get home you must take a single feather from the white eagle whose nest is in the high peak. Wear the feather wherever you go, and for as long as you wear it you will never fail in the hunt or suffer harm. Afterwards, you must carve a pipe for yourself. Each time that you smoke the pipe, the first puff will turn into a falcon .... And beware of your grandfather. He wants you only for himself."

The voice was beyond place, but it seemed to come from within an oak that stood to one side of the lodge's empty frame. While the young man was looking at the oak, the limbs and the branches faded from sight as if consumed by an invisible fire until the outline of an old man came into view, shaped from the trunk of the tree. Tree trunk from the waist down, he was rooted to the earth .... Then the vision vanished completely from before the young man's eyes.

Back home, the young man borrowed a feather from the white eagle and fashioned a pipe as he had been instructed. When he was ready to go on his quest a few days later, he told his grandfather, "Farewell. I will come back."

The young man had but one purpose: to destroy the giants. He set out towards the southwest. He searched among the sand dunes, believing that the giants were hiding among dunes on the north shore of Mishigameeng (Big Lake). He found no one. He crossed the country, looking into valleys and hidden caves along the way, until he came to the rocky shores of Kitche-Ojibway-Gameeng (Great Sea of the Anishnabeg). From Boweting (Place of Rapids), the young man followed the rugged shoreline wherever it wound or bent or curved. And he looked into every cavern, scaled every promontory, and went down into every hollow. In his journey the young man found the land not only beautiful but bountiful as well. Each day he ate something different: one night, venison; on another, whitefish; on the third, partridge and berries. But all the beauty and the richness of the land was in the possession of the giants. There were no Anishnabeg. The giants had to be destroyed.

But the giants were formidable. They knew the moment that the young man set out; they knew what his intention was. And they left him free to move about – another foolish man seeking self-destruction. They waited as a fox waits for a rabbit. Eventually, they would toy with him and watch him scurry to and fro, wanting to escape. Because of his own desperate efforts the young man would collapse. The giants would not need to resort to power or cunning.

After months of travel the young man finally came to the mountains which were the abode of the giants. From the peaks the giants watched him with contempt as he slowly scaled the slope. When at last he reached the summit, the giants welcomed him with warm smiles and offerings of food; but the young man refused. He had not come in friendship, he told them. He had come to test his powers against theirs in any contest of skill. At stake would be the loser's life.

The giants feigned surprise at the challenge, showing false concern for the young man. But when he insisted upon an immediate test, they settled upon a hunting contest. According to the terms of the contest, the hunter who caught the largest bear before sunset would be declared the winner. The hunters could hunt anywhere they chose and use any weapons, as long as they returned to the mountain before evening.

On his first hunting expedition, the young man killed a huge bear. It was much larger than that caught by his opponent, the youngest giant–and so the young man slew the giant. On four successive days the young man out-hunted his rivals, slaying the giants who had lost according to the terms of the contest. But the oldest and most powerful of the giants fled.

And so the young man went in pursuit of the last remaining giant. He crossed the marshes and the swamps of the Land of the Muskrat, coming at last to some lofty hills where he camped for the night. During his sleep, the young man's patron came to him in a dream with a warning: *Beware of the man.*

The young man went on. He travelled until he gained the heights of a mountain range where cliffs of rust and copper plunged steeply into gorges, and where deep valleys held rivers that gleamed like silver in the sun. He stood there and filled his vision with the immensity of the land and the sky. Looking down the trough of the valley below, he chose for his camping site a hook of land in the river. There might be fish in such a place.

Down in the valley he began to meet men and women of another tribe whose language he could not understand. The mountain valleys were the home of the Little Men of Metal. With each new meeting the young man smoked his pipe afresh, creating and releasing yet another falcon to show his power. The strangers regarded him with awe and wonder and let him pass. At last, the young man made camp. After a meal of fish that he speared in the river rapids, he lay down on a pallet of cedar boughs to consider what direction he should take on the next day. He was almost asleep when an old man emerged from the dark forest and offered to lead him to the place where the giant was hiding.

The young man agreed. But the guide was in fact the giant in disguise, and during the night he stole the young man's white feather and his pipe and changed the young man into a dog and himself into a fine warrior. Together, the warrior and the dog passed days on the trail in the mountain valleys. Finally they entered a forest where there was a small encampment situated at the end of an arm of land extending far into a lake.

At the encampment there were two sisters living together in one of the lodges. They were daughters of the chief, and they had chosen not to marry until the arrival of a warrior wearing a white eagle feather, as had been foretold in tribal prophecy. When the white-plumed warrior entered the village, the sisters went out bearing gifts, each hoping that the stranger would marry her. The stranger selected the older sister, and to appease the younger, gave her the dog.

Right from the first, things did not go well with the impostor and his wife. Believing that all he had to do was don the white feather in order to bring in game, the feathered warrior could bring back nothing from his hunting and fishing expeditions. In a short while his wife was finding fault with him, and the village hunters were scorning his techniques and his efforts. Meanwhile, the dog brought home all sorts of small game for the younger sister.

Unless he could provide some food for his wife, the impostor would be driven from the village by the laughter of the hunters. He would be regarded as less than a man, incapable and incompetent, a burden upon his wife and upon the village.

Certainly, it was humiliating to be outdone by a mere dog. On the next occasion when the dog left the village to go hunting, the impostor followed to observe what the animal did.

The dog went to the mouth of a small stream, just beyond sight of anyone from the village. There, he withdrew a flat stone that was about the size of a large moccasin, and the stone instantly turned into a beaver. When the dog carried off his catch, the impostor imitated the dog. He drew a rock from the shallows: it became a muskrat in his hands. He took another: two muskrats. With head held high, the impostor went home. From now on he could look the hunters squarely in the eye. He could provide for his wife as well as any of them .... When he reached his lodge he threw down the muskrats with a lofty air, but before his wife could pick the animals up they turned into stones. The impostor's shoulders sagged. He cast his eyes down.

Shrieking and calling names, the woman picked up the stones and hurled them at her husband. Her shrill voice rang throughout the village, and the impostor skulked away, her cries burning in his ears. He faded into the woods. But his wife could not endure the taunts and the laughter of the people of the village who had collected to witness the commotion. Unable to accept the unfitness of her husband and the foolishness of her choice she, too, slunk from the village.

When the impostor and his wife had fled, the dog, by motions, directed the younger sister to build a purification lodge and to assemble stones and water. Then he entered. During his enclosure, the vapours and the heat restored him to his original form. He emerged at the end of the purification period as a young man.

Although he was brought back to human form, the young man was without speech. Still, by motions, he made the villagers understand that they were to form a search party to track down the fugitives. A party led by the chief set out, and by evening they came upon the impostor and his wife setting up camp. The two of them were quarrelling.

Before any parley it was the custom to smoke a pipe. For use in the ceremony, the impostor offered the pipe that he had stolen from the young man. From the chief, the pipe was passed to the impostor who fixed the white eagle feather in his head band. The impostor puffed and sucked and drew upon the pipe like a leech. He would have smoked all the tobacco had not the chief wrenched the pipe from his grasp and handed it to the mute young man. Before he drew upon the pipe, the young man took the white feather from the impostor's head band and stuck it in his own. With his first puff on the pipe a white falcon fluttered out of the bowl in the midst of a blue vapour. Four more times the young man drew upon the pipe. Four more falcons were created.

And the young man recovered his voice. After the last warrior had smoked, the young man told the chief and the men of the annihilation of the Anishnabeg, and of how he had been brought to this land by his quest for the evil giants. Then he took his war club and with one blow felled the impostor ... the last giant.

In celebration, the chief ordered the performance of the War Dance of Triumph in the Festival of Victory. Just before the drum sounded, the chief addressed the village: "A great hunter and warrior has come among us. I invite him to be our brother and to take his place by our fire and to lead our hunters and to look after our people. He came to us as a stranger, nameless. I have seen his patron – a falcon that watches over him. I call him White Falcon, swift and sure. He is my son-in-law, our brother." And the chief turned to White Falcon. "Brother, you are welcome to our tribe."

But White Falcon could not remain. He already had a home that drew him, a force stronger than his newfound brotherhood. Before he left he promised to return often with his wife and sons and daughters, so that they could visit their grandparents and their other brothers and sisters.

THE NAMING

Cheengwun motioned to Waubizeequae to unlace the infant from the cradle-board. He closed his eyes as he pressed the child to his chest; and he held the child against him for a long time. This was the most solemn and profound moment in the ceremony. Cheengwun was about to give his N'Kweemiss a name. But first he was to give part of himself, to transmit a portion of his own potential to the child. There was no word for this potential; no word to describe its character; no word that could cause it to pass from one person to another. Because it was an act that was consummated between souls no words were necessary. Touch, flesh to flesh, was the way in which spirits met and became one. By holding his N'Kweemiss close, Cheengwun was letting part of his being enter the child. He willed his dream and his dream power to well out into the child to form part of the child's being and potential.

At last, Cheengwun opened his eyes. He held the child slightly away from his chest, and looked down at his N'Kweemiss. "Mishi-Waub-Kaikaik (Great White Falcon)," he said. "That is your name." He turned to the parents. "Mishi-Waub-Kaikaik is his name. It is a good name; it is a good dream." And Cheengwun handed Mishi-Waub-Kaikaik to his mother.

Afterwards, they feasted.

---

*The correct translation for the word *manitou* (as used, for instance, in *Kitche Manitou*) was not "spirit" but "mystery." The term could be applied to natural settings which had some special atmosphere about them, or to plants, whose powers of growth and healing were mysteries. It could also be used to refer to the men and women who possessed powers that could not be truly explained – for example, the men and women who became healers, and who understood the properties of the plants.

Tobacco Offering/
The Drum Ceremony

Peendaukoodjigewin/
Midewewegun

THE OFFERING OF TOBACCO

From his father's custom of burning tobacco at the onset of storms, of offering tobacco during journeys in those places deemed dangerous or sacred, and of implanting tobacco in the earth while gathering medicine, Mishi-Waub-Kaikaik learned that his people were always conscious of the presence of Kitche Manitou. Where that presence was greatest – at the top of a mountain, in a whirlpool, in a cave, on a small island, or in a cavern in rocks at the water's edge – the Anishnabeg would offer tobacco to the mysteries who abided there. The offering was given partially to appease, and partially to acknowledge a presence. For whatever reason the act was performed, it was always done with reverence and holiness.

No one knew when the practice began. No one could tell why it was tobacco that was used. But the practice was very old, and Mishi-Waub-Kaikaik learned a story about its origins.

Once there was a village – and beside the village there was a mountain whose summit was always hidden by clouds. Even on sunny days the cloud remained, and thunders echoed around the mountain top while lightning flashed in the skies. Thunderbirds were said to live on the mountain's crest.

In the village there lived a young man who longed to see the Thunderbirds, or even capture one; and he dared to think of scaling the mountain. He had no fear of Thunderbirds or the deities, and little regard for traditions that forbade anyone to climb the mountain and enter the domain of the spirits. He persuaded another young man to accompany him, and in preparation for the dangerous venture both went into fast for eight days.

On the ninth day, they began their ascent up the steep sides of the mountain. During their entire journey the rocks shook with thunder while lightning flashed and flickered. Near the final curtain of fog and mist the second young man refused to go further. Voices could be heard chanting above the mountain's rumblings.

Waegonaen maenaepowunt?
Waegonaen wauh pagidinigaessik?
Who dares without tobacco?
Who dares without offering?

Saemauh bizaundae/aekaugae.
Saemauh waussaeyaukaugae.
Tobacco will allay our anger.
Tobacco will clear the cloud.

Boldly, the first young man continued to go forward. As he disappeared through the mist he shouted, "I see them! I see them!" At the same moment there was a mighty roar and a blinding light. When the thunder died into the distance and the light faded, the mist that had covered the mountain was no longer there. In the next instant, the young man who had seen the Thunderbirds lost his footing and fell to his death at the bottom of the mountain.

Never again were thunders heard or lightnings seen on the rocky crests. The people said that the Thunderbirds had abandoned their nesting place and would no longer return. Their abode had been desecrated and they had taken revenge.

The same mountain sloped into a lake. Where it entered the water it formed a point; and this point, too, was covered by an ever present mist. Whenever anyone ventured near it, winds would suddenly rise and whip the waters into a mass of curling waves and currents. Many fishermen disappeared near the point and were believed to have drowned.

One day, the second young man who had climbed the mountain was paddling his canoe not far from the point when he was suddenly caught in a storm. The wind blew him directly towards the point. In his struggle to keep from capsizing he heard someone chanting sadly above the roar of the wind.

Apaegish abeedaubung.
Apaegish abeedaubung.
Oh! For the light of day.
Oh! For the light of day.

Apaegish ginopowauhingobun.
Apaegish zugussowauhingobun.
Oh! For the taste of tobacco.
Oh! For the smell of tobacco.

K'd powauguninaunind tikiziwuk.
K'd powauguninaunind tikiziwuk.
Our pipes are cold and empty.
Our pipes are cold and empty.

Through the fog, the young man observed a small canoe bearing several little people no taller than windflowers. Each passenger had a pipe, and it was their voices he heard singing.

K'gah baugwaushkaugameetchigaemim
Beenish mukwaenimikohing.
We will stir the waters
Until one remembers.

Saemauh beendae/aeshkaugae.
Saemauh beeninaendumishkaugae.
Saemauh bizaundae/aeshkaugae.
Tobacco cleanses my heart.
Tobacco cleanses my mind.
Tobacco brings calm.

Then the young man remembered how he and his companion had heard the chanting about tobacco on the top of the mountain; and even though he was in danger of floundering, he quickly set his paddle aside. He took the tobacco that he had with him and threw it into the waves. As the tobacco floated away, he chanted:

Saemauh n'weekaunaehn.
Saemauh k'weekaunaehnaun.

Saemauh k'weekaunissimikonaun.
Tobacco is my friend.
Tobacco is our friend.
Tobacco makes us friends.

The little people had not seen him, and they were startled by his chant. But they gathered the young man's tobacco from the waters and filled their pipes. As if by magic, their canoe glided away towards the steep cliffs where they and their craft disappeared into an opening that closed behind them. Immediately, the fog lifted, and the storm subsided. And even though the little people were never seen again, the Anishnabeg never forgot to offer tobacco to them in the places where they were thought to abide.

Thus began the custom of offering tobacco to the deities in their domains.

THE PRESENTATION OF DRUM

Mishi-Waub-Kaikaik's father had a drum that was encased in the finest buckskin and kept in a special place in the lodge. No one but Ogauh touched the drum. He only, by virtue of ownership and kinship, could sound the instrument. Such was the bond between man or woman and drum that the owner did not presume to transfer the instrument during life or to bequeath it to another at death. Tribal drums, however, were attributed with special powers, and were occasionally bestowed upon another tribe in an act of goodwill.

The drum presentation ceremony was not Anishnabeg in origin. Involved in wresting a living from their land of endless lakes and forests, and preparing, during the summers, to survive the long, harsh winters, the Anishnabeg were not a warlike tribe. A man's worth was measured, not by the number of eagle feathers in his head-dress, but by the number of deer and fish on his food racks. Success in the hunt was the result of his knowledge of the land, of the shifts of winds, and of the habits of game. It was evidence of his ability to endure in and with the seasons. For this endurance, men and women had to foster the self-reliance of both individuals and the tribe, and it was in this context that freedom and independence were valued and understood. But when the Anishnabeg had to fight, their warriors were the equal of any. It was from the Dakota, with whom they fought many battles in what is now Wisconsin and Minnesota, that the Anishnabeg received the ceremony.

For both the Dakota and the Anishnabeg war was a necessity, even though it disrupted the character of their traditions. As the Anishnabeg were dispossessed of their land to the east by the White Man, they retreated westward, and they, in turn, deprived the Dakota of their homelands. For five or six generations hardly a summer went by in which there were not battles between the two tribes. Against the more numerous Anishnabeg armed with rifles obtained from the White Man, the Dakota could resist only with bows and arrows, and they were forced to fall back. Finally, weary of bloodshed, worn in spirit, and wasted in numbers, both tribes sought to restore peace. And a story was told of how the way to friendship was revealed to the Dakota.

The two tribes, with many warriors on both sides, met and fought near a river. The wife of the Dakota chief had accompanied her husband, and at the start of the battle she hid in the river, covered by a large lily-pad. There, underneath the leaf, the woman remained in terror while the battle lasted.

After four days, a voice from the skies bade her come out. When she emerged from the river, all she could hear were moans of suffering and agony from the surrounding battlefield, where the earth was covered with the bodies of dead and wounded. Nearby, the surviving members of her tribe were preparing to head for home, and the woman was transported into their midst so that she could accompany her people.

One night, while her companions slept, the voice she had heard before summoned her to the skies. A sky deity addressed her. "If you are to have peace and friendship, you must seek it through the drum," the deity said. "It is a sacred instrument that bears goodwill and is a symbol of goodwill. He who gives a drum will both give and gain goodwill."

Before the woman was a drum and two drumsticks, a pipe and tobacco. As she watched they were transformed, and she saw men dancing around the drum and heard women singing.

Gawaekumoh n'meekunuh.
Gawaekumoh n'd'inaendumowin.
Gawaekumoh aenigookidae/aeyaun.
Gawaekumoh n'dinaudjim.
Straight is my path.
Straight is my mind.
Straight is my heart.
Straight is my speech.

N'gah zhawaenimauk n'dowaemauk, neekaunissuk.
N'gah zhawaenimauk waeseehnuk, binaehnssiwuk gayae.
Kind will I be to my brothers and sisters.
Kind will I be to beast and bird.

The deities told the woman that when she returned to the village she was to select two men for the making of the drum — and that after the men had made it they were to die. Then, the songs she had heard were to be sung by the owner of the drum every fourth day, to the offering of tobacco. In this way, the drum was to be imbued with ritual.

And so it came to pass. The drum was made under the guidance of the woman, and at its first sounding the two men who had made it fell dead, sacrificial victims for peace. Next, Misheen-Meegwun (Many Plumes), the Dakota chief, took possession of the drum. He appointed five keepers of the drum, a Keeper of the Drum Pipe (to be smoked by the drummers), a Keeper of the Pipe of Peace (to be smoked by the dancers), and a chief drummer and chanter. The chief also appointed four other drummers and chanters, eight women chanters, and four lead dancers. Every fourth day he visited the drum, offered tobacco, and sang the songs. At last, Misheen-Meegwun sent his courier to the Anishnabeg to offer friendship. The Anishnabeg accepted the offer, and a day and a place was set for the meeting of the tribes.

It was early afternoon and the sun was bright on the day when the two tribes advanced tentatively towards one another. The warriors were in their battle gear. Armed with war clubs, rifles, or bows and arrows, they uttered war cries.

Misheen-Meegwun sent his courier towards the Anishnabeg with a peace pipe. Accompanied by four women who walked back and forth singing, the courier presented the pipe to Neegaunaush (Sails in Front), the chief of the Anishnabeg. These were the Dakota songs of praise.

Ogimauh zoongigaubowih
Kauween w'dauh zhaugoodjigunaumaussee
Ogimauh zoongigaubowih.
The chief stands
He will not be struck down
The chief stands.

Ogimauhing
Bookissaenoon n'd'pigookimun
Tibishko aussimaupigauk.
Against the chief
My arrows break
As against a rock.

On receiving the pipe and hearing the songs, Neegaunaush motioned to his people to sit down. Sensing that there was something very special in the occasion, the Anishnabeg fixed their gaze upon the courier. Even the children suspended their prattling and stood still, waiting to witness whatever was about to take place.

Misheen-Meegwun advanced with deliberate, measured stride towards the assembly of Anishnabeg, the feathers in his head-dress brightened by the sunlight and swept by the wind. Lean and tall and stately, he stopped beside his courier.

"My brother!" he said, addressing Neegaunaush. "My brother! This day I wish to offer my hand and the hand of my people in friendship to you and to your people. Too long now have our people been at war. Our great grandfathers and our grandfathers fought, and you and I have fought. And what have we gained by our conflicts? It is not good for us or for our children to be constantly at war; always to be uneasy by night and ever wary by day. It was not intended by the Great Spirit that men should kill and wound one another; but rather that they should live in harmony as friends.

"The Great Spirit has given to us a drum as a symbol of brotherhood, and he has commanded us to offer you this instrument of friendship as a token of our goodwill. And the Great Spirit has instructed us in the proper custody of the drum and the manner of bestowing it upon other peoples. I now offer you this drum – and my hand – in friendship and brotherhood." And Misheen-Meegwun extended his hand to Neegaunaush.

The keepers brought the drum to a point midway between the two seated tribes. Next to the drum were placed the pipe and the two ceremonial drumsticks, side by side. Then the drummers took their places, followed by the singers and the dancers. At the stroke of the drum the chanters sang and the dancers enacted a dance of peace and brotherhood. They stopped on a signal from the chief drummer, who presided over the ritual.

Solemnly, the Keeper of the Drum Pipe then conducted Neegaunaush towards the drum. When they reached it, the keeper handed Neegaunaush the pipe and one of the drumsticks. Three times the Anishnabeg chief tapped the drum lightly. On the fourth stroke, the drummers themselves joined, the singers' voices carried across the sunlit meadow, and the dancers began anew. Afterwards, Neegaunaush took off his head-dress and presented it to Misheen-Meegwun. Then he, too, made a speech.

"My brothers! My sisters! Misheen-Meegwun is right. We have fought too often and for too long. Although we have gained honours from these conflicts, we have also suffered the loss of brothers and sons and fathers. It is time to hunt together, to celebrate festivals as one, to draw our meals from the same bowl, and to derive our warmth from the same fire.

"Our brother Misheen-Meegwun has never shrunk from battle, yet never has he shown greater heart than now. I accept the drum; and for as long as I have custody of the drum, my tribe will look upon the Dakota as brothers."

When the chief had finished speaking, the warriors of both tribes jumped to their feet, striking the earth with their war clubs and uttering shrill war cries. Then, leaving their weapons on the ground, they clasped hands.

That is how the Drum Ceremony began.

The Vision Quest

Waussaeyaubindumowin

THE INVITATION

"Come! It is time!" Ogauh said to his son.

At last it had come. The day for which Mishi-Waub-Kaikaik had waited and for which he had prepared had now arrived. He had thought about it so much that the edge of anticipation had gone. He felt no thrill when his father spoke. Instead, there was a fleeting moment of anxiety, almost of doubt. What if he were not ready? He was deemed ready ....

Come! It is time! That was all that was said. The time had come. Mishi-Waub-Kaikaik's time. The invitation was given as if it were a prelude to a meal or to some task as common as picking berries – something ordinary that was done every day. It did not seem like an invitation to enter upon perhaps the most vital of human ventures: the Vision Quest.

Ogauh's invitation signified that Mishi-Waub-Kaikaik had come of age to undertake the quest. He was fourteen. For the past eight years his father and his grandfather had prepared and instructed him for this event. By now, he understood the meaning of the quest and its obligations. He had come at last to his time. He was ready.

Still, Mishi-Waub-Kaikaik felt anxiety well up deep within him. He tried not to show it in front of the young boys and girls who gathered to watch the preparation outside the lodge. At first they watched without saying anything as Mishi-Waub-Kaikaik's face and arms and legs were blackened with ash. Then, as he picked up his bundle, one of the younger boys teased, "I hear there are lots of bears. Listen for their growls!"

But most of the others wished him well. "Be strong! There is nothing to fear! Your patron will look after you."

THE PLACE OF VISIONS

The Place of Visions was a long way from the village. It was a glade, a very small glade in the middle of the forest, circular and surrounded by tall pines. Its location was unnatural. The old people said that it was formed neither by man nor by nature but by some other cause: by Pau/eehnsug (Little Dwellers of the Forest). Such an origin gave the glade a mystic character. It belonged to the spirits who inhabited the earth. Here, far from men and women, they could preside over their affairs without disturbance. And the Anishnabeg respected the sanctuaries of the deities. These were special places. The only time that it was regarded as permissible to enter the domain of the spirits was during the quest for vision. On these occasions it was said that the spirits welcomed the visitor and aided in the quest.

Father and son entered the forest, leaving behind the clamour and commotion of the village, and were soon engulfed in silence and peace. They were no more than two shapes, images of one another, gliding among the beech and maple and other hardwoods, hurrying through the tranquil green spaces of the forest. There was no conversation between them, and no need to break the silence. They yielded to the quiet mystery of the forest's existence. By mid-afternoon they came to the Place of Visions in the very depth of the woods, where the pines and cedars and spruces grew tallest and thickest.

On their arrival, Ogauh placed an offering of tobacco in the centre of the circle. "Forgive us," he said. "Forgive my son. I bring him so that he may receive his vision. We ask that you be generous and grant him dreams." He was addressing the presence of the deities.

Before he left, Ogauh helped Mishi-Waub-Kaikaik construct a small lean-to with a bedding of cedar boughs. "I will come for you in four days," he reminded his son. "In the birch bark pail you have brought there is enough water for you. Be well .... And do not wander from this place."

SOLITUDE

Mishi-Waub-Kaikaik was left alone. He was totally alone for the first time in his life, and as he watched his father disappear into the woods he was not sure whether to feel joy or sadness in his isolation. He had longed for this moment, but now that it had come he had a sense of being abandoned. He shrank from it. A vague desolation of soul bore down upon him. He wanted to hear a human voice ... No, not that ... He wanted someone near, someone to lean on, to turn to ... But there was no one now. No one except himself.

How small was his world: the glade with only himself to inhabit it, sealed in on every side by immense pines and cedars! He walked around the perimeter of the glade without any particular purpose; and he was walking around his world. He tried looking beyond the wall of trees and underbrush, but his vision was limited. He heard the squawk of the bluejay and the knocking of the woodpecker and the calls of other birds – the only sounds that broke the silence. His surroundings dominated him. In everything, he was least.

Mishi-Waub-Kaikaik sat down. He could not understand why he felt uneasiness when he ought to have been at peace. Had he not received his instructions? Had he not thought about being alone? Had he not seen others leave the tribal fire and come back? Had he not mimed the quest many times in play? But leaving the encampment as he and others his age had done in imitation of their elders – leaving for an afternoon to sit alone in a cavern or atop a rock, always within range of the village – was not enough. They had always been encouraged to imitate elders in all things, especially in the performance of ritual that was the preparation for adult life. Mishi-Waub-Kaikaik had enacted the purification ceremony many times, as well as various other rituals, but they were only imitations. Blackening his skin with ash, no matter how many times performed or how perfectly done, had never been anything else but rehearsal; a solemn charade bereft of any essential element. All previous enactments of the vigil and the quest had been necessary as previews of the reality. For Mishi-Waub-Kaikaik, reality had now arrived. But he did not feel fulfilled.

For the rest of the afternoon, Mishi-Waub-Kaikaik's mind wandered back and forth between the present and the past – but when the dark began to take hold of the forest, stripping the trees of their colour and dimming their outlines, he concentrated on the past, where things were familiar. Then, as night fell, he could think only of the force of the dark and the depth of the silence and the edge of every sound in the stillness. All that he could discern in the pall of black were the forms of the trees above him and the stars in the height of the sky. Near and distant were alike. And yet, if his sight was dim, every other sense had sharpened, especially his hearing. It frightened him. He had heard these sounds before, many times, and he knew what they were; but always they had been heard from a distance and he had been safe within the shelter of his father's lodge. Next to his father and mother, Mishi-Waub-Kaikaik was not afraid. But now it was different.

A flutter of wings in the dark startled him and sent chills down his spine. The urgent whistle of a whippoorwill, unexpected and shrill, pierced the silence behind him, making him quiver. A little farther away, another whippoorwill whistled back in answer. *It's only a bird, harmless and small*, Mishi-Waub-Kaikaik told himself, over and over. But there were more sounds: beetles and crickets and frogs and other night creatures ... *They are only beetles and crickets and frogs, harmless and small* ... Still, Mishi-Waub-Kaikaik trembled. He could hear everything; see nothing. If only he could see, he would not be so afraid; everything would be all right. A little later he heard the sounds of breathing: quick and heavy, or shallow and short. He caught the crack of twigs as an animal ran by. With each of these sounds Mishi-Waub-Kaikaik stiffened, for he did not know what they were. After that there was the call of an owl and the bark of foxes and the high-pitched howl of a wolf. Mishi-Waub-Kaikaik knew these; but each rekindled his dread.

And then he remembered the monsters: the Weendigoes, Pauguk, the Nebaunaube who infested the forests. Mishi-Waub-Kaikaik felt a thousand eyes upon him; knew that a thousand ears were listening for him; felt the claws and talons and fangs ready to tear the flesh from his bones. And the

Pau/eehnsug! This was their domain. They were crowding and closing in upon him!

All Mishi-Waub-Kaikaik could feel was dread. He knew nothing else. It was cold – but he was not sensitive to the chill. His stomach ached – but he was indifferent to it. He was alone – but he did not move. Only his immediate safety mattered.

At last, the uncertain dawn arrived. The sky turned a soft blue, and the trees took on shape. During the slow transition from night to day, the robins and the vireos began to sing. Mishi-Waub-Kaikaik had survived.

SELF-DISCOVERY

Now that it was morning, Mishi-Waub-Kaikaik was relieved. It was true: he had survived. All the dangers and all the unseen foes that had threatened him throughout the night had vanished. He reflected; and the more he thought about his anxiety, the more he was ashamed of his fears and of himself. His fears had not been inspired by the owl or the fox or the whippoorwill – creatures who meant no harm, and who had awakened when others had gone to sleep only to come out and feed and talk among themselves as old men do. Instead, the fears had come from within himself, from within his spirit. And Mishi-Waub-Kaikaik ranged within his own soul in quest of the source of his fears. He found nothing; but he came to know a little of himself. He discovered things that he had not previously known because of his preoccupation with the activities of man and with the immediate and concrete world around him. He discovered things that would be hidden to others unless he revealed them. When he began to understand these things, Mishi-Waub-Kaikaik felt better.

Mishi-Waub-Kaikaik's spirit soared in the vast regions of his soul in which there was no time, no dimension. He crossed freely from past to present and even moved into the future. The sun was already high in the sky when he came to himself in the present, drawn back from the World of Soul by ache and discomfort. He had not moved for so long that his legs throbbed. Mishi-Waub-Kaikaik stretched and bent his limbs to ease the cramps. When feeling had been restored, he stood up tentatively, as a child rises to its feet and attempts walking by first testing the strength of its legs. He could walk, but his legs were weak. For exercise, he walked around his world, so finite and limited in comparison with the endless reach of mind and the ranging of spirit.

Then, as he stood beside his lean-to, Mishi-Waub-Kaikaik felt a dull ache in his stomach. Hunger. And he needed to drink. He took a swallow from the birch bark pail. Only a swallow – but it seemed to inflame his throat. He sat down. Far off, a flicker shrilled. Nearby, chickadees flitted nervously from branch to branch, restless, always in motion. They took his mind away from his pains. Mishi-Waub-Kaikaik looked down.

Below him was another world; the world of insects. He watched an ant struggle with a burden; behind it, another; and following, many others. One by one they disappeared into an anthill, emerging by another hole to return for another burden, so that there were two columns of ants: small, black, shiny beads moving between the blades of grass in an endless, silent cycle of labour. Mishi-Waub-Kaikaik picked one up, held it between his fingers, and watched it bend and twist its legs in helpless motion. With the removal of the ant from the column a gap was created, but only for a moment. The ants closed ranks as if it had never been. Mishi-Waub-Kaikaik put the ant back in between the columns. A space was opened, and the ant once more merged in the moving chain. All have a place. Each has a place willed, dreamed, and ordered into being by Kitche Manitou.

STRENGTH

Evening came and merged into night, and again the trees lost their individual colouration and shape, transformed by the dark into stark, blue-black shadows and dim outlines. There was a mist in the air and it was cold. The whippoorwills called. A great bird thrashed through the crowns of trees in flight. A fox yelped. For Mishi-Waub-Kaikaik, all these things had now lost their fearful aspect. They were no longer threats,

48

but merely sounds; the voices of animals and birds in talk.

There was something else for him to think of as he lay huddled in his blanket at the end of the lean-to. The cold. He shivered in the dank mist that moistened everything. He curled his body for warmth, but that brought only fleeting relief. With the cold, came hunger. Mishi-Waub-Kaikaik longed for meat, for warm broth, for a handful of dried corn, for anything to allay the fierce tearing in his stomach. He ached in every limb and joint and sinew; there was a pain in his eyes. He was sleepy but he could not sleep. Oh! Comfort! Warmth! Ease! A full belly! Every part of his body demanded relief. For most of the night, Mishi-Waub-Kaikaik was conscious only of the physical discomforts that overwhelmed everything else.

When daylight came, Mishi-Waub-Kaikaik realized what was happening. Concentrating, he drove out his body's desires. He could not let them govern his spirit, for it was the spirit that must be dominant, regulating all human needs. This was mastery of self; the beginning of a new existence.

Although he was sleepy, Mishi-Waub-Kaikaik did not sleep. He fought the heavy drowsiness that lay upon him. Now, on this third day of his vigil, he was calm. There was no urgency to see anyone, because everything was there if he chose to dwell upon it. He could permit his spirit to transport him to times he had never lived, or to worlds he had never seen. Yes, his spirit took him to the worlds in the sky, opened his ears to sounds that he had never heard, and let him understand those sounds and find them beautiful. And he came to know his soul and to form a vague notion of his spirit. But it was too elusive for his mind to hold – like the twinkle of a firefly in the night which is there like a blue-yellow bead, only to vanish the next moment, appearing again in yet another place.

Mishi-Waub-Kaikaik heard it before he saw it .... He looked up into the late afternoon sky. There, high in the clear blue was an eagle, its wings motionless, held up by columns of air and wafted in circles by currents and eddies and whirlpools of wind. It was as light and graceful as a canoe. "Ah!" Mishi-Waub-Kaikaik thought. Were he to possess the vision and the swiftness of the eagle, he would see farther and run more swiftly than any man. Were he to possess the ferocity of the eagle, to do brave deeds, he would wear the eagle feathers upon his head. He could daunt the enemy …. The eagle drifted higher and higher until it faded.

But that was selfish. In those thoughts there was too much of self, too little of others. While the vigil was conducted alone and the quest was for revelation of self, Mishi-Waub-Kaikaik knew that he must return to the tribe of which he was a member and live out his vision in and for the tribe. The tribe came first, not in an abstract sense but in the concrete: the aged and the children and those to come – all the people. And yet the tribe coming first did not mean that the individual was to live only for the tribe, to serve only others. If he could say, *I am the first of men; I am the last of men*, and mean it and prove it with and by deed, then, and only then, would he be worthy, fit to serve the tribe. For this, Mishi-Waub-Kaikaik had been counselled and trained. But to put self totally above and beyond the people was against tribal belief and practice. He must not think of it.

THE FIRST VISION

As the last night of his vigil arrived, Mishi-Waub-Kaikaik stopped his struggle against sleep. He closed his eyes, falling asleep immediately, but his spirit was alive and vibrant. It took him into the skies, past the moon and the sun and beyond the stars, until he came into the presence of the sky spirits, the patrons of music and echoes. One of the sky spirits conducted him to a lodge of rainbow where the attendants removed his clothing. Next, he was led to a purification lodge. Afterwards, they gave him new clothing.

The sky spirits were talking, but Mishi-Waub-Kaikaik didn't understand. No words were spoken; there were just signs and the dialogue of looks and glances. Mishi-Waub-Kaikaik followed his guide to a third lodge, one made of stars. Looking in the entrance he saw a drum, a flute, and a root inside. Then the guide led him back to the first lodge. All around them were other lodges of the same colours and hues – but they were of many different shapes. Some were dome-shaped, others peaked.

Mishi-Waub-Kaikaik sat down. He gazed upon the lodges of

Odjeeg-Anung (the Fisher Star) and Waubun-Anung (the Morning Star) and Ningobi-Anung (the Evening Star), and as he looked, he began to chant. As he chanted, he began to understand the voices of the sky spirits, and his voice mingled with theirs.

N'daebaub auzhiwi-anungoong,
K'gah kikinowaezhigook anungook.
I can see to the other side of the stars,
The stars will guide you.

N'daebitum auzhiwi-anungoong,
K'gah noondaugook anungook.
I can hear the other side of the stars,
The stars will hear you.

Kaugigae n'gah daebitaugoos.
Timeless is my voice.

Soon, all the stars – red stars, women stars, and distant stars – were joining in the singing.

K'gah waussae/aubindum nebau/in,
K'gah gawaek-oshae nebau/in.
Even in sleep you will perceive,
In sleep you will hear.

Ae-naubindumun dah izhi-waebat,
K'zhawaenimik Kitche Manitou.
What you dream will be,
The Great Mystery is generous with you.

Maukinauk k'gah mizhinawae/ik,
Tchi mino-dodomun, k'bawaudjigae.
Through the turtle will you speak,
For good will you dream.

Nindo-waewaemishinaung.
Call us.

The songs echoed away, and the guide touched Mishi-Waub-Kaikaik and motioned for him to go. Slowly, the lodges of stars and of rainbows faded from view .... And a second dream began.

THE SECOND VISION

From the sky, Mishi-Waub-Kaikaik was transported back to earth. There, a young boy ran up to him in tears. "He has taken him!" the boy cried. "He has taken him! Get him back! Get him back!" Pleading, the young boy tugged at Mishi-Waub-Kaikaik's sleeve.

"Who?" Mishi-Waub-Kaikaik asked.

"My little brother. A Weendigo has taken him!"

And Mishi-Waub-Kaikaik set out in pursuit of the monster. After several days he caught up to the Weendigo, and in a terrible battle, slew the giant with his club. Strapping the baby in its cradle-board to his back, Mishi-Waub-Kaikaik then started homeward.

But already the brothers of the slain Weendigo were in pursuit of him. Warned by a woodpecker that his enemies were gathering and were now close behind him, Mishi-Waub-Kaikaik ran. At first he ran easily, but eventually the cradle-board upon his back grew heavier and slowed him down. Soon the Weendigoes would be upon him! In desperation, Mishi-Waub-Kaikaik hid the cradle-board in a small cave that he found, asking the bear within it to care for the child and to return him to his family. Then he ran on, but now he moved even slower than before. Utterly exhausted, he finally fell.

Mishi-Waub-Kaikaik was thirsty and choking. There was no moisture in his mouth. A swallow of snow was all that he needed and it was there, under him, all around; but so weak was he from running that he could not turn his head or move an arm to scoop up even a handful of snow. A stranger passing by saw Mishi-Waub-Kaikaik lying on the ground and, guessing his need, carried him to a nearby lake that was covered with thick ice. Using his hatchet, the stranger hewed a well and gave water to Mishi-Waub-Kaikaik. As soon as Mishi-Waub-Kaikaik was able to move and to help himself, the stranger hurried on.

Mishi-Waub-Kaikaik drank and drank and drank – but he could not quench his thirst. He kept his mouth in the water and finally entered the lake through the well, continuing to drink until he had drained the lake and had swollen in size. When he stood up, he shattered the ice – just as the Weendigoes arrived. When they saw him, they fled.

This dream was immediately followed by a third.

THE THIRD VISION

There was a large crowd of people standing on the shore of a wide lake, waiting for the wind to die down so that they could launch their canoes and begin their migration to another land westward. They were a poor people. Their tools were made of stone and wood; their garments were of skin; their bedding was made of boughs and their lodging of bark. Their only valuable possessions were the necklaces and brooches that the women wore. These were made of shells.

The land around the people was also poor. Game and fish had gone, and the yield of berries and fruits was small. Because the people did not have enough to eat, they had decided to kindle their campfires elsewhere. And they had chosen to go to the west, to the Land of the Setting Sun. They had heard that this country was as fair as the evening shadows, and that the earth there was bountiful. Now they were impatient to start.

Even as they waited on the shore, the people were quarrelling and grumbling. They were not a tribe, but a collection of peoples who had come together more by chance than by choice. Now they were disagreeing about whether they should strike to the southwest or to the northwest, and about all kinds of other, petty matters.

Finally, they asked Mishi-Waub-Kaikaik to lead them. But he had no experience in leading and showing the way. A trout was leaping on the surface of the lake, and Mishi-Waub-Kaikaik asked it for direction. "Will you guide us to the Land of the Setting Sun?" he asked. And the trout agreed.

For seven days and seven nights the migrants travelled westward, following the trout, before they came to the western end of the immense lake. There they camped. But the people did not believe that this was the Land of the Setting Sun. It was too poor and dull compared to the horizon. And so, by the third day, the people were again grumbling. "Let us go on! Why are we waiting? There is nothing here." Mishi-Waub-Kaikaik questioned a fox who had come near the camp. "Will you lead us to the Land of the Setting Sun?" he asked. And the fox agreed.

The people trekked westward through thick forests until they came to the plains. No further would the fox go. The people camped there for two days, but they knew that this was not the place. It was too flat, too barren.

Mishi-Waub-Kaikaik next persuaded a buffalo to guide the people across the plains. It took them ten days, and then they came to mountains beyond which the buffalo would not go. And though the mountains shone white in the mornings and pink and red in the evenings, they were too cold and too high. The Land of the Setting Sun must be beyond.

And so Mishi-Waub-Kaikaik asked a mountain goat to conduct them over the mountains. Along the way they met strange tribes whose language they could not understand and whose food they could not eat. At the bottom of one large mountain the migrants sat down, disheartened by the height of the peaks. They complained about Mishi-Waub-Kaikaik. They refused to go further unless he found them food and carried them out of the high, rocky places. With the help of many mountain goats, Mishi-Waub-Kaikaik led the people to the end of the mountains and the edge of a great sea. From the shore they looked out to the horizon, and they knew that they had still not reached the land they were seeking.

But the people travelled on. They journeyed northward, led by a snow goose, to a land bound by snow and ice. Still, they were no nearer to the Land of the Setting Sun. Abandoning their quest, the people returned to their own country. Never again did they regard their home as poor.

THE MEANING OF THE VISION

When Mishi-Waub-Kaikaik woke up, his father had already arrived with some meat and dried corn and cold water. It was the fourth day of fast. Mishi-Waub-Kaikaik was weak; but he felt refreshed.

"Aneehn! You must be hungry," said Ogauh, greeting his son. He set a bowl of food in front of Mishi-Waub-Kaikaik, and although he was no longer hungry, Mishi-Waub-Kaikaik ate. And the food tasted good.

Afterwards, they walked slowly home, stopping frequently along the way to rest because of Mishi-Waub-Kaikaik's weakness. He told his father, "I think I had a dream." That was all he said. His father only nodded.

When Ogauh took Mishi-Waub-Kaikaik to Cheengwun, the medicine man, for an interpretation of the dreams, Cheengwun confirmed that it was a vision and that Mishi-Waub-Kaikaik need go out no more. Nevertheless, Mishi-Waub-Kaikaik did go out. But although he dreamed again, his dreams differed little from the first three.

Later, all his visions came true. The water that he dreamed represented long life. Mishi-Waub-Kaikaik lived for ninety-six years. The trek across waters and plains and mountains, where the people looked to him for direction and food, symbolized leadership. Mishi-Waub-Kaikaik was chief of his tribe for more than twenty years. Finally, the chanting sky spirits or deities signified the gift of prophecy. As a member of the Midewewin, Mishi-Waub-Kaikaik could invoke the sky spirits for knowledge of the future on behalf of a petitioner.

When Mishi-Waub-Kaikaik invoked the sky spirits, the success of the ritual depended upon the faith and the integrity of those present. The ritual was known as the testing. If the conditions were right—if there was nothing in the preparations or in the minds of those attending the ceremony to mar the petition—then the voices of the sky spirits could be heard. Their presence was shown by the shaking of the lodge.

Mishi-Waub-Kaikaik was a Jeesekeewinini (One Who Communes With Another World). When he summoned his patrons in the sky, he was heard to chant in a different language—and some who heard him said that he was using a language very old and long ago forgotten.

The War Path

Baunindobindidowin

THE PURPOSE OF BATTLE

The Anishnabeg were primarily men of peace, visionaries who depended upon hunting for survival. Since the worth of a man was measured by his generosity and by his skill in the hunting grounds, bloodshed was not the final test of manhood in Anishnabeg society. Instead, the War Path was followed when it was deemed necessary to avenge an injury, whether real or imaginary, to oneself or to one's brother. It was a matter of pride never to let insult or injury go unpunished – but never was conflict begun for the purposes of conquest or subjugation. The frequent use of ritual during Indian war expeditions emphasized the fact that a battle could be seen as a sacred mission.

Battles between tribes were thus essentially the result of a need for revenge. They seldom involved a large number of warriors and, because they were similar to hit and run raids, they rarely lasted beyond half a day. Conflict was personal, rather than tribal, and it was undertaken with a fierce sense of duty. It was because of this devotion to the avenging of wrongs, with no regard for consequences, that warriors were feared.

THE INJURY

One of the fiercest warriors in Mishi-Waub-Kaikaik's village was Bebon-Waushih (Flying in Winter). One summer, news came to the village that there had been a raid on a neighbouring encampment and that three people in that camp had been killed. One of these people was Bebon-Waushih's sister.

Within moments of hearing the news, Bebon-Waushih had but one purpose: to avenge his sister's death. Had the warriors of his village been home he would have recruited a war party immediately, but they were away and would not be back for several days. Until they returned, he would have to wait.

Brooding, Bebon-Waushih continued the necessary activities of hunting and fishing – but the only thing he truly nourished was the resentment that welled in his blood. Grief and sorrow and bitterness blended to produce a pain that dulled his mind and his senses but gave an edge to his resolve. Only revenge would relieve the hurt.

The elders of the village offered sympathy and tried to dissuade Bebon-Waushih from carrying out any reprisals against the enemy. From long experience they knew that taking one life to avenge a first would only result in more deaths and the creation of more resentment. But even as they gave their counsel they knew that it was futile. It was a point of honour for Bebon-Waushih to settle the score with the killers of his sister. According to tribal belief and custom, the soul of a victim had been separated from existence both in this world and the next by the act of malice perpetrated against it. Ill will had rendered the soul an outcast from the Land of the Living, and its own turmoil made it an outcast from the Land of Souls. Only retaliation could console the spirit and restore it to the community of departed ancestors. What Bebon-Waushih wanted to do was sanctioned by belief and practice.

CONSULTATION

Before the hunters returned from the hills, Bebon-Waushih went to Baeshkwae (Night Hawk) a medicine woman. He told the old woman that he was going to raise a war party to avenge his sister's death, and requested Baeshkwae to advise him on the outcome of his expedition. And Bebon-Waushih offered tobacco for the performance of the Shaking Tent Ceremony for revelation as to the results of the War Path.

Then he went to Mishi-Numae (Great Sturgeon), the chief of

the tribe, to ask permission to take up the war club. It was not always necessary to do this, but it was better to let the elders know about plans for war. More than likely they would deny his request, but there was always the chance that they might sanction the expedition. If the elders of the tribe did indeed consent to the risks of war, it would be easier to raise a party of men.

When he heard the request, Mishi-Numae looked at Bebon-Waushih for a long time, communicating both disbelief and disapproval of the plan. Finally, the chief said that he would discuss the matter with his advisers, and he asked Bebon-Waushih not to do anything until he heard from the council.

After a few days, Bebon-Waushih was summoned by Baeshkwae. She had communed with the sky deities on his behalf. The spirits had replied: The kingbird overcame the crows; the kingbird overcame the hawk; and the kingbird overcame the eagle. It was a good omen, she said. A sign of triumph. Bebon-Waushih understood it to mean that he, too, would triumph.

But the chief and the elders were opposed to war. They would not sanction it. They said that it would only lead to more hard feelings and bloodshed, and would undo all the years the tribe had spent living in peace with the other tribe. Moreover, since the offense occurred in another village, it was really no concern of theirs. It was true, Mishi-Numae pointed out, that the tribe could not prevent Bebon-Waushih from pursuing his course. But the elders were not going to support him, or encourage any others who might join him in his adventure.

Tribal objection did not matter to a war chief as strong willed as Bebon-Waushih, although consent would have made it easier to recruit warriors. Still, there would be some men willing to accompany him, especially the young ones eager to win honours for themselves and establish themselves as men of courage. Since it was the hunting and fishing season, Bebon-Waushih would probably have to take some of these untried young ones to complete his war party. It would be a risk – but Bebon-Waushih had decided that he would need at least eight or ten men.

WAR MEDICINES

Now Bebon-Waushih returned to Baeshkwae, to ask her to prepare war medicines for the expedition. No raiding party went without these medicines. If the party was of sufficient size, a medicine man was invited to accompany it and attend to the warriors with a supply of medications. They were all powerful potions.

The first medicine was the Bizhikeeibuk, the buffalo root which conferred strength and endurance. So potent was it that a drinker unaccustomed to its strength had to build up his capacity by stages, until he could endure four draughts daily. Four times a day, a warrior was required to prepare and drink the strength-giving elixir. Into a small birch bark cup filled with water he would dissolve a small quantity of powdered Bizhikeeibuk. Then, taking the cup in his hands and closing his eyes, the warrior would proffer the cup to the north, the east, the south, and the west, petitioning the deities who dwelled in the four corners of the earth to give him strength. *Let my strength be like that of the mighty buffalo who rock-like withstands the prairie blizzards and fiery days. Like the mighty buffalo let me be tireless on the trail so that if need be I could walk around the world.*

The second medicine was the Minissinowushk, by some called the island medicine, by others the warrior medicine. It was applied to a wound to staunch the flow of blood.

The third was the Waubunowushk, a medicine that was prepared by a member of the Society of the Dawn and encased in a small bundle to be carried by a warrior. It was believed to possess mystical powers, and could both protect the bearer from harm by negating the bad medicine of the enemy, and overcome the enemy's own protective medicine. Such was its power that it was believed to be as important as the bow and arrow or the war club. Warriors who survived many battles were said to possess the Mystery of Continued Life. This gift of the Great Spirit – which every warrior and every man and woman longed to receive – was embodied in the Waubunowushk. The medicine man would preside over the Waubunowushk with prayers, petitioning Kitche Manitou to pass the mystery of survival and life through the Waubunowushk to the warrior.

THE INVITATION TO WAR

Sometimes, the war chief would send his courier to invite warriors to take part in his cause. But usually this was a task he preferred to perform on his own. Personal appeal was always more persuasive than that delivered by a messenger. Either way, the petitioner had to follow form, a form as old as the tribe itself.

After requesting the preparation of war medicines, Bebon-Waushih began to invite warriors to join in his expedition. He went to Beewaubik (Iron), a warrior who had won many honours and who had gone on many previous raids. They sat cross-legged on the ground across from each other, Bebon-Waushih talking quietly, Beewaubik tracing images in the sand. Yes! He would go to inflict pain and grief and help settle accounts. The word given, Bebon-Waushih lit the pipe, the red Pipe of War, and handed it to Beewaubik. This was the way of sealing a pact, a solemn recognition of a pledge that was not lightly given. It was totally binding. Unless a man could fulfil his word he did not make a promise; but once he gave his word he was bound to keep it. To be a man was to be one whose word was trusted.

Beewaubik blew four puffs of smoke from the pipe and called upon the deities to bear witness.

Keenwauh ayaubeetumaek keewaetinoong
Mishishuh n'zugusswauh.
To you who abide to the north
Before your eyes I smoke the pipe.

Keenwauh ayaubeetumaek waubunoong
K'ginoonikoom tchi noondumaek.
To you who abide to the east
Before your ears I speak the word.

Keenwauh ayaubeetumaek zhauwunoong
Kaugigaenig n'd'kittowinun.
To you who abide to the south

63

Beyond your distance my word echoes.

Keenwauh ayaubeetumaek epingishmook
Mishiwigeezhigoong n'bazawaewaeshin.
To you who abide to the west
Beyond time my word endures.

Then Beewaubik finished smoking the pipe in silence.

Bebon-Waushih went on. Of the six leading warriors in the village whom he wanted, four agreed to come: Nawadjiwon (In the Middle of the Stream), Mee/auwaussige (Directly Shining), Aupita-Geezhig (Half Day), and Zaugitau (Emerging Bud). Two others declined: Maudji-Geezhig (Moving Sky) and Manitouwaub (Sees Like a Spirit). They would have liked to go, but they had already arranged to take their families picking blueberries. Perhaps, they said, there would be another occasion. Bebon-Waushih regretted that they could not come. They would have added force and experience, and they had powerful medicine. But to refuse was their right; it did not cast doubt on their courage. It was a matter of priorities, something that no one questioned.

As Bebon-Waushih moved from point to point in the village, he discovered that everyone knew of the impending raid. Most were opposed to it. It seemed that the only ones who were in favour of the raid were the young ones: boys of sixteen or seventeen years of age who wanted to be men, who wished to reach the next stage in life by performing an act of manhood. Belonging neither to boyhood nor to manhood they were still not deemed fit to go with the men on their raids. Their medicine was neither tasted nor tried. But, as Bebon-Waushih had expected, there were many who begged to accompany him. Finally, he agreed to take four youngsters. With only five men his force would be small; but with five men and four boys – and the medicine man – there would be ten in all. One of the boys Bebon-Waushih chose was Mishi-Waub-Kaikaik.

The date of departure was decided. The night before, the village would conduct the War Dance.

THE WAR DANCE

Assisted by the four boys, Bebon-Waushih cut a fresh cedar

post which he implanted in the middle of the village circle. This was the War Post. Then, with a crowd of smaller boys and girls to help them, Mishi-Waub-Kaikaik and his companions gathered wood for the war fire. The rest of the village was busy preparing halves of fish, cuts of venison, corn, and berries for the meal that night.

When the sun sank beyond the hills, the four boys kindled the pile of wood they had gathered. A lone drummer began to chant in a high-pitched voice and to drum slowly and plaintively. It was a summons; but many people were already there, waiting to watch and to listen. This was a solemn occasion; for all a farewell, for some (especially the younger ones) a spectacle. More sticks and branches were flung into the fire. The lone drummer continued. Soon, four more drummers arrived, walking in single file behind the Drum Keeper. He tested the resonance of the drum and adjusted the pitch by exposing the face of the instrument to the heat of the flames. To the west, the clouds were purple. Upon the hills, the forests were of the same hue.

Then the drummers, four of them, began tapping the drum. They beat gently at first, almost tentatively, as if afraid to disturb the silence or to injure the drum; but then, reaching unison and rhythm, they struck the drum harder, until it echoed into the shadows and beyond. The whippoorwill and the owl were silent, and the insects suspended their singing before the beating of the drum. The drumming, hard and insistent, went beyond words to evoke a primordial instinct. Echoing in the shadows of the night and in the depths of the soul, the drum could move men to passion by sound alone. And the drummers were intense as they kept the rhythm and the pitch constant. Their minds were fixed on the drum. When a high-pitched voice began to come from the throat of the first drummer, the other drummers soon followed, all of them chanting without words.

With two light taps the lead drummer changed the tempo of the drumming to a slower, more measured beat. There was no chanting now, just the rhythm of the drum. Led by Bebon-Waushih, a single file of warriors emerged from the dark in full regalia. They wore their head-dresses and armbands and amulets, emblems of their courage and their deeds; they wore loin cloths, leggings, and moccasins. In their hands they carried war clubs. As they entered the area lit by the war fire, they began to dance.

Four times they danced around the fire, brandishing their war clubs, tilting their heads back to yelp in war cry. Twisting and bending and coiling their bodies, they wove about the flame. After they completed the last round, they sat down facing the War Post.

The war chief, Bebon-Waushih, went to the War Post. He stood in front of it, facing his warriors and his audience, and every eye was upon him. He was tall and lean. He was lithe as a fox. And he moved with the grace of a deer, suggesting agility rather than brute strength. His eyes were like those of a hawk, piercing and all-encompassing. The head-dress that he wore had fifteen plumes, each representing a triumph. Rising straight from the head band, they made him look even taller. As the village watched, Bebon-Waushih raised his war club.

"My brothers! My sisters! My totem and my family and I have been given a great injury. Indeed, the tribe itself has suffered harm. We all suffer equally when a member of the tribe dies. There is one brother less in our family and in our totem; there is one member lost to the tribe. My sister ... our sister ... was killed in the village of our tribal brothers in our own land. Not only has the enemy injured my family – but it has scorned our tribe by attacking a village of our brothers and sisters in our own land.

"Are we to let this bloodshed stand? No, my brothers! We must not allow the enemy to enter our territory in order to beset our brothers and sisters and wave their war clubs in our faces. They will regard the Anishnabeg as no more than crows who are cowed by every small bird in the sky. Our safety is threatened! Our courage is at stake! I, for one, will not allow a member of my totem or of my tribe to be harmed without redress.

"It is not for nothing that I belong to the wolf totem, the totem of those who are warriors and guardians of the tribe. It is not for nothing that I wear these plumes and these armlets, gained in defence of our people and our villages. I am a peaceful man – but I am not afraid of war! For you and for our children I have risked my life in the past. I now risk it again."

66

While he was talking, Bebon-Waushih moved back and forth in front of the War Post brandishing his club. He began to recount his war deeds for the benefit of his warriors, especially the youths going out for the first time. This was the only occasion on which a warrior spoke of his exploits.

"On my very first expedition, a long time ago, Book-Iningaweengun (Broken Wing) was my war chief. Our war party walked many days before we came upon the camp of the enemy. It was larger than we had expected. They had more than fifty warriors. We had but ten. Outnumbered, we could not storm the camp; and so we waited in hiding, keeping watch on their movements. On the fourth day our scouts saw four of the enemy coming from the north. We hid on top of the ridge; the enemy walked below in the gully. We could not see them; but neither could they see us. They were talking and laughing so that we knew where they were. When they were just below us Book-Iningaweengun gave a signal, and we rushed upon the warriors. Being young and quick, I reached the enemy first. I leaped upon the one walking in front. Before he could raise his war club I struck him down!" And whirling, Bebon-Waushih sprang upon the War Post and smote it viciously, as if it were an enemy's skull. "Before he lay still, I had my knife out. I cut a portion of his scalp. On that day I became a warrior—entitled to wear an eagle feather, to go with men. During the celebration of the Festival of Victory, Book-Iningaweengun presented me with my first feather.

"On the second expedition under the leadership of Book-Iningaweengun, we challenged the warriors of the enemy camp to open battle. They were eight. We were ten. But they came out; and we fought together with clubs. During the fighting I saw one of the enemy raise his club and rush upon my war chief. I pursued him, and before he could strike I seized him about the waist and called to Book-Iningaweengun. Book-Iningaweengun slew the man while I held him—and for holding an enemy warrior I wear this armband, given to me at our Victory Dance." Bebon-Waushih pointed to a strip of skunk skin that encircled his left upper arm. Then he coiled and sprang and clubbed the War Post.

He went on to a third account. "On yet another occasion, my fellow warriors tested me. They asked if I had the courage to hold the standard in the middle of the battle ground during the fight – and I did. I held the standard and taunted my enemies and dared them to wrench it from my grasp. I stood my ground as I was expected to do, to give my life if necessary for the emblems of the tribe. My fellow warriors knew then that my medicine was strong and that my heart was strong; and the enemy knew it also. And this armband," Bebon-Waushih pointed to a skunk skin on his right wrist, "is proof of my courage on that occasion." He struck the War Post again.

Bebon-Waushih continued to tell the story of his deeds. It was a long account, even though it was but a summary of each of the warrior's fights. He did not embellish his stories. He did not have to, for he was telling the truth. He spoke of himself and about his deeds; but he was not boasting. Bebon-Waushih was recounting fact. When he had finished, he stared fiercely at the assembly around him. "My brothers and sisters! That is what I have done. And that is what I will do." Striking the War Post a final blow, he sat down.

Nawadjiwon, second to Bebon-Waushih in number of battle honours and next in rank, got to his feet as Bebon-Waushih sat down. He was a thick-set man, especially broad across the shoulders, moose-like in appearance and in movement. His face changed as he recalled and relived his encounters with the enemy, describing how in his very first fight he let slip his war club, and unarmed broke the neck of one of the enemy and choked a second to death; how on another occasion he had to act as a decoy to distract the enemy; and how yet in still another battle he ran into the enemy's midst and came out with only a cut arm and a few bruises. He showed the enemy his medicine. Nawadjiwon recounted ten more feats, striking the post thirteen times in all. He was followed by Beewaubik, Mee/auwaussige, Aupita-Geezhig, and Zaugitau, all of whom told of their victories.

Then it was the turn of the youths who Bebon-Waushih had chosen to go on their first war expedition with him. When Mishi-Waub-Kaikaik got up he was embarrassed that he had no tales to tell. Untried, he could not recite any deeds of valour or daring – but still he danced and struck the War Post with as much force and ferocity as he could command. He was determined to prove himself a man of strength and courage, and hoped that he would perform well on the battlefield so that later he could, like Bebon-Waushih, recount the story of his own exploits.

All four of the young men danced and struck the War Post with their clubs; and when they sat down, one of the older men of the tribe came into the circle of the fire. The man was carrying a small, white, mongrel dog. Barking, the dog jumped to the ground to snatch at a piece of meat that had been flung before it, and then sat on its haunches, waiting for another piece. But the old man, taking a knife from his belt, caught the dog and slit its throat in one swift motion. The animal went limp, eyes rolling and legs jerking; and in the next instant, the old man slit its stomach, quickly extracting the liver. He put the bleeding, red-brown liver on a block of wood and cut ten strips. Starting with Mishi-Waub-Kaikaik, the youngest of the aspiring warriors, the old man made the offering of a strip of raw dog meat. Mishi-Waub-Kaikaik took the strip of meat, looked at it for a moment, and then put it in his mouth. He did not flinch – for that was the way. Whoever took part in the Dog Feast was expected to eat the meat without cringing. It was an act of courage to see a dog killed and then to eat its flesh; but to draw back or to disgorge the dog's liver was the equivalent of cowardice. All of Mishi-Waub-Kaikaik's companions and all of the warriors ate the meat without flinching. The warriors looked as though they had partaken of dog meat many times before, and would have eaten more had there been a greater supply.

During the Dog Feast, there were some children and women who recoiled. But when Bebon-Waushih, the last in line, ate his portion, the members of the tribe shouted "How! How! How!" in acclamation.

And the drumming resumed, more intense and more solemn than before. More wood went into the fire, making the sparks fly upwards to blend with the drifting smoke and vanish into nothingness in the night sky. Then, Bebon-Waushih led his warriors around the fire. It was not a dance he led, but a re-enactment of his previous conflicts. It was an outpouring of his passions: hostility, pride, contempt, daring, fear, courage, sadness, triumph – every emotion finding expression in

69

his eyes and in his voice and in his violent yet graceful motions. On the fourth circuit around the fire all the rest of the tribe joined in, not in sanction of the venture, but in the spirit of brotherhood. On and on they danced, bodies dripping with perspiration, not stopping until Bebon-Waushih sat down. The drummers put away the drum. And the entire tribe feasted on the food that had been prepared.

THE JOURNEY

In the morning, the war party left the village in single file as a small crowd of early risers gathered to watch them depart. In front of the war party were four women, walking back and forth, blocking the path of the warriors, imploring them to return home. But this, too, was ritual. No pleas would stop the warriors. Nothing could. At last, the four women ran ahead a short distance, where they stood facing one another, two on either side of the path. Between them, the warriors passed.

It was four days by foot to the nearest enemy camp; four days' walk through forests and swamps, across streams and rivers. There would be eight days or more of anxiety for the tribe. An old woman who had seen the Northern Lights even before Bebon-Waushih had determined upon revenge, said that its pink-red hues, flashing from the top to the bottom of the heavens and staining the skies from side to side, represented the flowing of blood. This prophecy would bear heavily upon the minds of the tribe while the warriors were gone.

For the warriors there was no such foreboding. Did they not possess good medicine? Experience? Courage?

On the first night, they made a small camp near a lake. The older men constructed shelters from cedar boughs while the youths, Mishi-Waub-Kaikaik and his companions, speared fish for their evening meal. Before they ate, Bebon-Waushih warned the young men never to step over the weapons of a warrior that had been set side by side on the ground near his shelter. To do this would be a bad thing, since youths who were untried in battle might negate the mystic medicine of the weapons. And he instructed the young men to arrange their own weapons in order and to respect them in the same way. Moreover, Bebon-Waushih assured the young men that after

70

the coming battle they could place their war clubs beside those of warriors.

At sunset, Bebon-Waushih and all the warriors drank their Bizhikeeibuk. Afterwards, Bebon-Waushih took his small rattle and sat down cross-legged facing the southwest, the home of the enemy. The five experienced fighters sat behind him, while the four untried youths placed themselves even further back. Softly, quickly, Bebon-Waushih shook his rattle, humming deep in his throat before breaking into his war song.

Zhawunoong, zhawunoong
N'd'muwihnaegae, n'd'muwihnaegae.
To the south, to the south
I go to cause them grief, I go to cause them grief.

Keewaetinoong, keewaetinoong
Tibishko n'gah naningishkowauk, tibishko n'gah
 naningishkowauk.
Like the north wind, like the north wind
I will make them quake, I will make them quake.

Mishi-kineu, mishi-kineu
N'd'gawautaeshkauk, n'd'gawautaeshkauk.
The mighty eagle, the mighty eagle
Overshadows me, overshadows me.

N'd'pugumaugun, n'd'pugumaugun
W'd'gawishkaugaemigut, w'd'gawishkaugaemigut.
My war club, my war club
Will fell someone, will fell someone.

Apee waubumuk, apee noondowuk
N'gah wukaunkaunauh, n'gah wukaunkaunauh.
When I see him, when I hear him
I will make him slave, I will make him slave.

Myeengun n'dodem, myeengun n'dodem
Naneezaunizih, naneezaunizih.
The wolf is my totem, the wolf is my totem
Dangerous is he, dangerous is he.

Wauss-Nodae, Wauss-Nodae
Misqui-geezhig, misqui-geezhig.

71

The Northern Lights, the Northern Lights
Blood was the sky, blood was the sky.

Meegwauhnse, meegwauhnse
Bemaushih geezhigoong, bemaushih geezhigoong.
A feather, a feather
Is flying through the sky, is flying through the sky.

N'zaesaegawaudjigun, n'zaesaegawaudjigun
W'dah bimissae, w'dah bimissae.
My amulet, my amulet
Will take flight, will take flight.

Kogaediwinning, kogaediwinning
W'dah muhwiwuk, w'dah muhwiwuk.
In that village, in that village
Many tears will flow, many tears will flow.

Kauween n'zaegizissee, kauween n'zaegizisee
Wauweendung nibowin, wauweendung nibowin.
I am not afraid, I am not afraid
Of the mention of death, of the mention of death.

N'mushki-akeem, n'mushki-akeem
Aupitchi-manitouwun, aupitchi-manitouwun.
My medicine, my medicine
Is very potent, is very potent.

Keenwauh, keenawind
K'minissinowim, k'minissinowimim.
You, we
Warriors you, warriors we.

One after the other the warriors chanted their war songs in the dark by the small fire; all except the young men who sat at the back. And the echo of the chants faded into the skies. Afterwards, they performed the War Dance again, not with the same intensity or with the same clamour, but with the same depth of purpose. At the end of the dance they again drank the powerful Bizhikeeibuk.

In the morning, just before setting out, Bebon-Waushih presided over the Pipe of War Ceremony. It was a simple thing, much like the Pipe of Peace ritual, except that the purpose of smoking was to petition the deities and the patrons for their protection during the journey and in the forthcoming battle. Every day the warriors had to perform the same acts: smoke the Pipe of War, take the Bizhikeeibuk, celebrate the War Dance, chant their war songs, and set their weapons in a certain way.

On the last evening, the night before the battle with the enemy, the attending medicine man prepared a blood-red solution in a birch bark bowl. Bending over the mixture, he said prayers and sang songs.

Tibishko beewaubik
Pugumaugun, pugumaugunun.
Like iron
The war club, the war clubs.

Tibishko waussmohwin
Pigook, pigookoon.
Like the speed of lightning
The arrow, the arrows.

Then the medicine man turned to the warriors. "Ahow!" he said. "My brothers! Dip the points of your arrows in the medicine. Stain them. It will make your arrows true and swift." Beginning with Bebon-Waushih, each warrior dipped the point of his arrow in the solution, and each time the medicine man repeated: "Red as the colour of blood. Red as the colour of blood." When the arrows had been dipped, the same process was repeated with the war clubs.

During the previous three days, the warriors had taken the Bizhikeeibuk silently. Now, on this last evening, Bebon-Waushih sang a chant.

Tibishko mishi-kaikaik
N'baeshowito, acthinahwito.
Like the falcon
I shorten distance, compress time.

Auzhigo n'waubumauh
Gawissaet, gawissaewaut.
Already I see
Him fall, them fall.

Bebon-waushih, n'd'igoo

Bebon-waushih, n'd'igoo.
They say I fly in winter
They say I fly in winter.

Kauween n'gah bimiwaugunaezissee
N'gah geewae.
Without a wound, unmarked
Will I go home.

To one drinking the Bizhikeeibuk, all distance would be alike as it was for the falcon – not in terms of speed but in terms of stamina. The powerful war medicine gave strength. As he drank the Bizhikeeibuk, Mishi-Waub-Kaikaik recalled his own patron, the white falcon, and felt eager for the fight and confident of his return home.

THE FIGHTING

The next morning, after the war party had smoked the pipe, Bebon-Waushih sent two scouts ahead to search out and spy upon the enemy. The main body of warriors slipped through the forest, their faces painted in red and black – the colours of war and death.

It was around midday when the scouts, who had been a mile ahead, came back with a report that they had seen the enemy. They reported that there were a great many, too many to be attacked. A whole tribe was on the move. All that afternoon the warriors stalked the column of migrants, waiting for stragglers. But none appeared. Then, late in the afternoon, the migrants forded a river and set their camp on the other side of the water. While most of the enemy was busy pitching lodges and preparing the camp, several small parties of men left to go hunting.

From the cover of willows, Bebon-Waushih's warriors watched as three men armed with spears came down to the river. At the bank the men looked upstream and downstream, and after a brief discussion, turned upstream. The war party followed. Eventually, the three men forded the river at a rapids. Just above the rapids was a small lake with banks that fell steeply into the water. Each of the men took up a position at a different point along the ledge, waiting, spear poised for fish. And the war party approached.

The steady roar of the rapids muffled all sounds that the Anishnabeg might have made. They moved quickly, stealthily. Like lynx they crouched, and like lynx they sprang forward at the fall of Bebon-Waushih's hand. It was over in moments. There was hardly a sound. There was no time for the enemy to cry out or to offer defense against the blows of war clubs. When the bodies lay bleeding and prostrate on the ground there was the bright flash of knives as three scalps were taken. Afterwards, there was no triumphant war cry to celebrate victory – only swift, silent departure.

CELEBRATION

At sunrise on the next day, Bebon-Waushih sent Mishi-Waub-Kaikaik ahead to deliver news of the victory, to assure the tribe of their return, and to prepare for the War Dance of Triumph. Mishi-Waub-Kaikaik had been one of the first warriors to leap upon the enemy, and he was elated as he went ahead, feeling certain that he had won the right to no longer be considered a boy. Following behind him, the warriors also travelled quickly, sustained by the Bizhikeeibuk.

When the day came on which they approached the tribal camp, the warriors began to whoop, letting the people know that they were home. Hearing the war cries, the women of the village, led by Bebon-Waushih's wife, went out to meet the men. They laughed and talked all the way, and upon meeting the returning party, Bebon-Waushih's wife took the scalp hoop to which the three scalps were affixed.

Back in the village centre, the scalp hoop was attached to the top of the War Whoop Pole, and then the pole was erected where the War Post had stood. While men and women began to gather wood for the fire and to prepare food for the feast, the children gathered about the warriors, eager to hear about the enemy and the activity of the battle and to discover whether the youths who had gone out had proved themselves. Yes, they had. They were now entitled to wear a feather and to walk with men and warriors. They had gone out boys, returned as men.

It was late in the evening, the sun just disappearing beyond the rim of distant hills, when the medicine men and women came to the War Whoop Pole. They set the wooden images of the tribe's totems on the ground: Chejauk (Crane), Noka (Bear), Myeengun (Wolf), Numaebin (Sucker), Migizi (Eagle), Addikmeg (Whitefish), Addik (Caribou), Peepeegizaence (Sparrow Hawk), and Muzundumo (Black Snake). Dressed in their finest head-dresses, leggings, and tunics, the medicine men and women sat in a circle about the images. A drum beat and a voice chanted as the Pipe Bearer uncovered the Pipe of Peace and gave it to Bebon-Waushih, who was sitting with the elders. The pipe was lit with a coal.

One after another the elders smoked the pipe, blowing whiffs of smoke upon the images of the totems. The warriors had brought peace upon the village, and blowing upon the totems was a way of commemorating the peace that would now descend upon all the families of the tribe.

When the pipe returned to Bebon-Waushih he held the bowl of it in his right palm and the stem in his left. Closing his eyes, he, too, began to chant. He began to rock the pipe, slowly and gently at first, and then faster and faster until his hands were almost a blur as he made the Puwaugunugauwin (Dance of the Pipe of Peace). Gradually he checked the motion of the pipe, and then passed the pipe to his right. From one elder to the next the pipe was passed, each time going through the motions and the rhythms of the dance. It was by making the Pipe of Peace dance and share in the triumph of the people that the tribe celebrated all great events. Always, the sacred pipe was first. On its return to Bebon-Waushih for the second time, the war chief handed it to the Pipe Bearer, who put it away.

Bebon-Waushih spoke. "My brothers! My sisters!" he said. "Today, we celebrate victory. But before we celebrate, let us honour our warriors!"

The tribe answered: "How! How! How!"

"Let us also honour the youngest and the newest men among us. They came with us as boys; they returned with us as men. They are now entitled to wear the eagle plume and to take their places among warriors." And beginning with Mishi-Waub-Kaikaik, Bebon-Waushih presented each of the young men with a feather.

As the feathers were presented, the people continued their shouts of praise and acclamation. And afterwards, everyone danced to the throb of the drums.

76

The Marriage Ceremony

Weedigaendiwin

THE NATURE OF MARRIAGE

The Anishnabeg word for the relationship between a man
and a woman was "weedjeewaugun," meaning companion – a
term which referred equally to male or female. There was no
distinction in sex; no notion of inferiority or superiority. More
particularly, "weedjeewaugun" meant Companion on the
Path of Life – "he who goes with" or "she who walks with."
For both men and women, a companion was someone to walk
with and be with through all aspects of life and living. Such
was the notion of marriage: the taking of a companion. It was
the strongest of bonds.

For the Anishnabeg, a woman's worth was not measured
by a lithe body, an unblemished complexion, full breasts, or
sensual lips. How well she cooked, how well she sewed – or
even the nature of her temper – were the things that counted in
a woman. How many deer or fish he could find his family,
and how frequently he could provide them, were the stand-
ards for a man.

COURTSHIP

Mishi-Waub-Kaikaik's parents had chosen a wife for their
son, with the agreement of the young woman's parents. But
the young woman died, and Mishi-Waub-Kaikaik was twenty-
five before he himself considered marriage. When he mentioned his wish to his mother, she told him of the industry and
the good nature of Manitou-Meenaehnse (Spirit Berry), a girl

who lived in another village. Waubizeequae urged her son to visit relatives who lived in the same village, so that he could see the girl for himself.

The journey took three days. When he reached the camp, Mishi-Waub-Kaikaik visited for a time with his relatives, and he saw that Manitou-Meenaehnse was an attractive girl who was praised by everyone. Eventually, he went to the lodge of Missaubae (Great Being), Manitou-Meenaehnse's father.

When Mishi-Waub-Kaikaik walked into the lodge, Missaubae motioned for him to sit down at the back, the place for guests. "There must be something," he said, looking up.

"I want to marry Manitou-Meenaehnse," Mishi-Waub-Kaikaik told him.

Missaubae continued to unravel the lacing of a snowshoe that he was repairing. He acted as if he had not heard, as if he resented any intrusion upon work that was more important than any other consideration. But his deliberation was customary. It did not come from misunderstanding, or from any disrespect for Mishi-Waub-Kaikaik's time. The Anishnabeg often took days, weeks, or even months to think about some matter before giving answer. They had long experience with the consequences of instant decisions. Even though an urgent issue, or another person's needs were involved, it was always better to take time.

There were many practical reasons for "taking time," but dominating them all was a reverence for "the word." To be asked to make a decision was to be asked to give "word," an awesome request. An answer or decision was final; a pledge, irrevocable and binding upon him who pronounced it. It was an extension of someone, a test of "being true." Keeping word was the measure of a person's integrity. When Missaubae was asked to pass his daughter to a young man he did not know, he could not decide in an instant.

"I do not think she is ready," Missaubae said finally, speaking deliberately as he unbound the mesh of the snowshoe. "She is of age ... but I do not think that she would make you happy. You would blame us. And that would not be good. Instead, you should be happy with her, and say that we taught her well." He paused. "She should stay home until she

80

learns how to cook and sew and keep the lodge clean. She should know all these things by now ... like the other girls here. Maybe you should ask for one of the other girls."

"I want to marry Manitou-Meenaehnse," Mishi-Waub-Kaikaik repeated.

"Maybe you should look for someone else. It is only Manitou-Meenaehnse's mother who makes certain that I do not wear torn coats and moccasins, and that I do not have to cook my own meals ...."

Now, what Missaubae was saying about his daughter was not true. He was testing Mishi-Waub-Kaikaik, who was a stranger from another village. By pretending that his daughter had no skills, Missaubae might discourage this outsider.

"But," said Mishi-Waub-Kaikaik, "I heard that she was skilled."

"I do not know what you heard," answered Missaubae. "She is hard to live with ... like a badger. Maybe one day she will hurt someone unless she controls her temper."

"I heard that she was cheerful," Mishi-Waub-Kaikaik persisted.

But Missaubae would not make a decision.

The next day, Mishi-Waub-Kaikaik returned to the lodge with a deer that he left at the entrance. When he did this he said nothing. The deer was an offering, a proof of his skills. A few days later, he brought another deer to the lodge. Two in a week. Surely, he was a good hunter. On this second occasion, Mishi-Waub-Kaikaik spoke again to Missaubae.

"I still want to marry Manitou-Meenaehnse," he said.

"If you feel the same way about her next summer," Missaubae answered, "then you can come back."

"Yes," said Mishi-Waub-Kaikaik. "I will come back ...."

THE NEED FOR PRUDENCE

Missaubae and his wife Neezhigeezhigoquae (Two Sky Woman) questioned their daughter, and found out that she was interested in the hunter from another village. It might not be a good thing for Manitou-Meenaehnse to prefer an outsider to a member of the tribe. There could be trouble. Rejected suitors

81

were known to have whipped young women, or to have harmed them by going to a sorcerer for medicine and the performance of a ritual that would summon up evil spirits. It was unlikely that Manitou-Meenaehnse would have done anything to offend anyone. She had been trained well. Still, there was no harm in offering her counsel.

"Someday," Neezhigeezhigoquae told her daughter, "you, too, will have daughters. You must watch, as I have watched. And you must tell your daughters what I will tell you. Remember. There are young men in our own village ...." And she told Manitou-Meenaehnse a story.

Once there was a girl named Wauh-Oonae (Whippoorwill). When she was young she was brought up by a stepmother who taught her nothing, and the people of her tribe thought that she was lazy. Only when her stepmother died did Wauh-Oonae discover that she could not look after herself. By that time, all her friends were married. No one would look after her. She was lonely, and she was poor.

Afraid that she would never be able to look after herself, she went to an old woman who taught her how to sew coats, leggings, dresses, moccasins, and gauntlets. After a while, Wauh-Oonae could make garments better than anyone else. Many people came, some from distant villages, to acquire clothes that she had made.

At first, Wauh-Oonae accepted whatever was given to her in payment. Then she began to demand more meat and hides for each of her coats and dresses. She asked for more and still more. Young men came to her lodge asking to marry her, but not one of her many suitors was good enough.

Then something happened to her hands. They grew stiff at the joints and Wauh-Oonae was no longer able to sew. Some said that one of her suitors had gone to a sorcerer who caused her joints to grow stiff. Others said that she had abused her gift by exacting a price for it. She ought to have shared the Great Spirit's gift with others.

From her hands, the stiffness spread to the rest of Wauh-Oonae's body, and there was nothing that the medicine men and women could do to save her. During the illness, an old woman in the village mentioned that she had heard about a spring of life-giving water. But it was far to the west and no one knew the exact place.

A young man who had been rejected by Wauh-Oonae offered to get the life-giving water. While he was gone Wauh-Oonae got worse, until she was lingering on the edge of death. At last the young man returned with a small pail of water .... And after Wauh-Oonae drank the water – said to give both life and generosity – she recovered and married the young man.

THE NEED FOR ACCEPTANCE

Manitou-Meenaehnse listened to her mother's story; but she still preferred Mishi-Waub-Kaikaik above the young men of her own village. When she mentioned to her mother how tall Mishi-Waub-Kaikaik was and how lean, Neezhigeezhigoquae warned, "Never judge a pine by its lines." She related another story.

In the old days, it was the custom for a tribe to marry off a young girl to an old bachelor during the annual corn harvest. The girl to be married was the one who found a warped red kernel among her husked corn. There was much excitement at the corn harvest. No woman wanted to draw the warped kernel for it was considered unlucky. Often the young woman ended up with a man no one wanted. One year, Bigaunaehnsequae (Small Seed Woman) drew the warped kernel. All the other young women laughed in relief at their own good fortune. And they laughed at Bigaunaehnsequae, who had to marry a deformed old man.

In the fall, the tribe left their summer encampment to go to their winter quarters. During the trek, Bigaunaehnsequae had to look after her husband, who was lame and had to use a cane. Although Bigaunaehnsequae's sisters told her to leave her husband behind, she refused and stayed by his side. At last there came a day when the old man lay down, unable to continue, and the rest of the family went on ahead. The old man closed his eyes as if he were dead, and Bigaunaehnsequae wept over his body through the night. In the morning, her deformed husband was no longer there. Instead, before her was a young man, straight and strong. He told Bigaunaehnsequae that he was the old man. He had been made old and deformed by a sorcerer.

The young man and Bigaunaehnsequae hurried to catch up with the family and the rest of the tribe, but along the way, Bigaunaehnsequae was struck by the sorcerer's spell. By the time they caught up with the family she was old and blind. She begged her husband to leave her behind as she was now a burden upon him and upon her family, but he refused to go. He would stay by her side as she had stayed by his. She was his companion and he would not leave her.

Bigaunaehnsequae grew more and more infirm, and for the last part of the journey the young man had to carry her. He had just finished building their winter home when Bigaunaehnsequae closed her eyes and died. Grieving, her husband also died; and he accompanied his wife along the Path of Souls until they arrived in the Land of Souls together.

THE NEED FOR JUDGEMENT

While Missaubae and his wife were counselling their daughter, Mishi-Waub-Kaikaik had returned home to tell his parents how pleased he was with Manitou-Meenaehnse. Waubizee-quae was glad; but to remind her son that the young woman's industry and good nature were more important than her looks, she told him a story.

There was once a young man who went looking for a wife. He left his own village because none of the women pleased him, and he travelled farther and farther until, in a distant tribe, he found a yellow-haired woman of great beauty. He married her – but he soon found that he had to do all the cooking, sewing, and mending, otherwise there would be nothing to eat and no clothes to wear. Before long, the man's wife began to change. The hair that had been yellow as corn faded, turned white, and fell from her head. The body that had been lithe grew thin, so that her clothing seemed to droop about her bones. No longer beautiful, and unable to perform the simplest of tasks, she was a burden upon her husband. Secretly, he packed his belongings and stole away from her side in the middle of the night. He had married Dandelion.

THE DECISION

Mishi-Waub-Kaikaik was determined to return to Manitou-Meenaehnse. In solitude, he sang his love songs.

Kauween baekaunizid
Keen aetah k'bishiigaenimin.
I care for no one else
I care only for you.

Kego kishkaendigaen
Kego muwihkaen
K'gah abi naunin.
Do not be sad
Do not cry
I will come for you.

Paumauh abi-izhauminaun
N'gah bizaum-odae/ae
N'gah bon-inaendum.
Only when I come to you
Will my heart be at ease
Will my mind be at peace.

In late summer, Mishi-Waub-Kaikaik passed through Manitou-Meenaehnse's village with a party of warriors. Although he did not come to her family's lodge, Manitou-Meenaehnse saw him from a distance; and when she was alone, she, too, sang a love song.

Tibishko peedauniquok, w'gee abi-izhauh
Tibishko waebauniquok, aubidji-maudjauh.
Like a cloud has he come and gone
Like a cloud gone forever.

N'kishkaendum w'gauh abi-ako-izhaut
N'kishkaendum w'gauh ako-maudjaut.
Sad am I since he came
Sad am I since he's gone.

N'gee mukowik
N'gah abi naunik nah?
He has found my love
Will he return for my love?

W'naugozih tibishko anung
W'waussuh waendaugozih tibishko anung.
Like a star within my vision
Like a star beyond my grasp, my love.

The next summer, Mishi-Waub-Kaikaik returned to Mani-tou-Meenaehnse's village as he had promised. By now, Mis-saubae knew something about the young man who wanted his daughter, for he himself had made a trip to Mishi-Waub-Kaikaik's village. Still, more testing had to be done. In order to prove himself, Mishi-Waub-Kaikaik brought much game to Missaubae's lodge over the period of a month.

Finally, Missaubae asked his daughter if she wanted to marry Mishi-Waub-Kaikaik. When she agreed, the date of the marriage ceremony was set. On that day, only Manitou-Mee-naehnse, her parents and grandparents, and the immediate family were in the lodge. As they sat about the fire, Mishi-Waub-Kaikaik's place was next to that of the young woman he was about to marry. A feast and games were to follow the marriage, and outside, the people of the village waited for them.

Within, the grandparents were to perform the ceremony.

THE NEED FOR LOYALTY

"Remember!" said Manitou-Meenaehnse's grandmother. *"Always help each other – just as Omeemee helped her companion."*

Waub-Addik (White Caribou) had wandered for many years before he was admitted into one of the tribes on the shore of the Great Sea of the Anishnabeg. He erected a lodge on the outskirts of the village where he lived alone, hunting and fishing to provide for himself. One evening, he returned home late from hunting to find his meal prepared, his lodge clean, and his pipe ready. Who had cooked? Who had set his home in order? The questions bewildered him. The same thing happened on the next two nights. On the fourth night, Waub-Addik could only stare at the food as if he were numb. He began to suspect sorcery.

Then a young woman entered his lodge. "Why do you seem

so sad?" she asked, as she sat down. The two of them talked for a long time. Waub-Addik learned that her name was Omeemee (Pigeon), and that she lived on the far side of the village with her parents. About midnight, she left.

The next evening, when Omeemee returned, Waub-Addik asked her to marry him. Omeemee agreed, but when she invited Waub-Addik to meet her parents, she warned him that despite their smiles they were evil. If Waub-Addik remembered her at all times, and did whatever she asked, then he would suffer no harm. Omeemee assured him that she possessed greater powers than those possessed by her parents, and that as long as he trusted her he would be safe. Before Waub-Addik left for her parents' lodge, Omeemee told him to deny that he had ever met her.

When Waub-Addik came to the entrance of the lodge, he was welcomed by Omeemee's father. "We knew you were coming," said the old man. "And we know why you have come. You must have met our daughter, Omeemee."

"I have not met anyone," Waub-Addik replied, remembering Omeemee's warning.

"I find that strange, indeed!" the old man remarked. "Yes, it is strange that you should want to marry our daughter without knowing her." He studied Waub-Addik closely. "You can have her – if you can do what we ask of you. We need to be sure that you can look after her."

Waub-Addik agreed.

On the morning of the next day, the old man took Waub-Addik deep into the forest. With a sweep of his arm he told Waub-Addik that he was to strip the bark from the birch trees, gathering enough for the construction of twenty lodges and twenty canoes. The task was to be done by nightfall. Before he left, Omeemee's father handed a small quill to Waub-Addik, telling him that this was the tool he must use to strip the bark. When he was left alone, Waub-Addik did not even try to do what he knew to be impossible. He sat down, buried his face in his arms, and wept.

Then he heard a woman's soft, kind voice. "Did I not ask you to think of me? Did I not assure you that I would help you?" Omeemee stepped from between the trees. "Did you forget me so soon?" she asked. "Or did you think that I was too weak? Never forget that for many things in this life, two are needed." And Omeemee cradled Waub-Addik's head in her lap and stroked his forehead until he fell asleep. When Waub-Addik awoke, Omeemee was gone—but around him were great bundles of birch bark. Every tree had been stripped.

At nightfall, the old man returned. Seeing the bundles of birch bark he frowned. "I do not think that you have done this," he said. "Someone must have helped you. But there is still another task. Tomorrow, I want you to drain a small pond."

But the pond was not small. There was a stream flowing into it and another flowing out. To drain it, the old man gave Waub-Addik a wooden ladle. Again, the task was to be finished by nightfall.

There was nothing more hopeless. For the second time, Waub-Addik burst into tears; and for the second time he was comforted by Omeemee's soft voice. "Foolish man! Have you again forgotten me? Yes, this is impossible for one person—but do you not remember that for many things, two are needed? Do you not know that we must help one another? Did I not promise you?"

Sitting by the pond, Omeemee washed Waub-Addik's hair and sang him a song.

K'weedjeewin
Tibishko mong punae cheega/eehn.
I am by your side
Like a loon, always nearby.

Waub-Addik slept. Later, when he woke up, the pond was completely dry. The stream that had emptied into it was now dammed by a beaver.

"Someone must have helped you!" said Omeemee's father, as soon as he arrived at nightfall. "You could not have drained the pond by yourself. Did my daughter do this?"

"I did not see her," replied Waub-Addik.

"Well ... I have only one other request. If you can catch enough fish by tomorrow night to last me for the winter, you can have Omeemee. I will make no other demands on you." The old man handed Waub-Addik an awl. "You must use this," he said. "It is the only spear I ever use."

When he faced his task the next morning, Waub-Addik gave way to tears and despair. Again Omeemee came and consoled him with sleep. It was late in the afternoon when Waub-Addik awoke, and he was astonished by the immense quantity of trout and whitefish that was spread to dry on racks. The old man, too, was astonished; but he said that he was satisfied. That evening, Waub-Addik and Omeemee were married.

During the night, Omeemee whispered to Waub-Addik that her mother was more dangerous than her father and that it was better for them to leave. They slipped quietly out of the lodge and into the night. "As soon as they learn that we have gone, my father will come after us," Omeemee warned. "Look behind once in a while. When you hear and feel an icy wind and see a dark shadow you will know that he is coming. Let me know. It will give us time to conceal ourselves."

When Omeemee's mother woke up, she discovered that her daughter and her son-in-law were gone. She blamed her husband for the loss of her daughter, and sent him to bring the girl back and to kill Waub-Addik. The old man set off, and soon began to gain on the fleeing pair. From the icy wind and the dark shadow that went on before him, Waub-Addik knew of the old man's approach. He told Omeemee, and she changed her husband and herself into pine trees.

The old man went home without seeing them; but the old woman was so furious at his failure that she would not let him back in the lodge. Enraged, she sent him out to search once more for their lost daughter. Even though Omeemee and Waub-Addik had gone quite a long way, the old man again overtook them with his speed. This time, the couple just managed to escape by becoming partridges.

Now the old woman went out to hunt them down. Omeemee had warned Waub-Addik that this would happen, and to escape her mother the two of them became a pair of loons swimming in the middle of a lake. But they did not deceive the old woman. From the shore she recognized them easily, and called out to them, threatening. But the two birds flew away, avoiding her power and finally finding freedom.

As in Omeemee's song, it was the close companionship between loons that best reflected the union between husband and wife.

THE NEED FOR KINDNESS

"Remember!" the grandmother said. *"Be kind to one another. And after the children come be kind to them, and they will be kind to you in your old age. They are of our tribe."*

A man and woman were very hard on their youngest son. The man beat him frequently, while the woman found fault with everything that he did. At last, unwilling to endure any more abuse, the little boy ran away. He was soon hopelessly lost in the forest, and the thought that no one cared for him made him cry.

"Why are you crying?" asked a bear, discovering the boy among the trees.

The little boy fainted from fright, afraid that the bear would kill him. But when the animal stayed near him only to guard him from harm, the fear turned to friendliness. Soon he began to trust the bear who brought him food and kept him warm at night, and after a while he was calling the bear "grandfather," while the bear called him "grandson." In time, the boy forgot his parents and his brothers and sisters.

During the entire summer the bear taught the little boy everything about the forest. The boy learned what foods to eat and what not to eat. Always, the two of them took care to avoid villages and hunters. Once they stole some fish and a box of honey from a cache of food, but they only sat down to eat it when they had hidden deep within the forest. In the fall, the bear was very fat from all the berries and fish that he had eaten. Knowing that it was time to sleep and rest, the bear found a den where he and the boy slept all winter. Not once, in all their wanderings, had the bear become angry with the boy.

Back at the village, the mother wept while the father searched day and night for the son who had disappeared. Finally, believing the boy to be dead, the family put black on their faces in mourning. An old medicine woman asked the father and mother why they were putting on such a show of grief, since they had given little care to their son and had driven him away by their harsh treatment. She said that they ought to be glad for the little boy, who was safe and happy where he was now. The parents' sorrow was even keener – but it was too late.

With the coming of spring the bear and the boy emerged from their den. At first there was hardly enough food to sustain them. Men, the bear remarked one day, were also in need, and if it were not for the care of the boy, he would offer himself to help the people. But the little boy did not understand. As berries ripened and the days grew warmer there was more to eat. The days ought to have been carefree, but something was bothering the bear. Often after a meal he would sit, staring into the trees as if he saw an event and was holding it there.

One morning at the end of summer the bear told the boy that he must return to his parents. "Since you left, your mother has not smiled, and your father has not known a happy moment. They will not abuse you again. They need you. That is where you belong. Come, grandson! I will take you home."

The boy cried all the way, dreading the memories that rushed upon him, and full of a sense of loss at parting from his grandfather. The bear led the boy to the shore of a lake. There he left him with the words: "Grandson! If ever you or your people are in need – call me!" And he vanished into the forest.

Soon afterwards, some hunters found the boy and took him back to the village and his parents. He was welcomed with a great feast, and everyone regarded him with a mixture of fear and awe because he had survived a winter in the forest. From the moment of his return, the boy received nothing but care and affection from his parents.

Later that fall, the boy went hunting with his father. As they were paddling across the lake to the hunting grounds, they saw five bears in the water. The boy called out, "Grandfather! Feed us!" And with the meat from the bears the family ate well all winter.

When she had finished her stories, Manitou-Meenaehnse's grandmother sewed the hems of the coats of Mishi-Waub-Kaikaik and Manitou-Meenaehnse together in marriage. She spoke the ritual words.

Taubishko boodawaun.
You will share the same fire.
Taubishko gawiwiniwaun dauh goodaenoon.

You will hang your garments together.
K'gah auskodaudim.
You will help one another.
Taubishko k'gah nauguhdoom meekunnuh.
You will walk the same trail.
K'gah naunaugata-waendim.
You will look after each other.
Mino-dodaudik.
Be kind to one another.
Mino-dodowik k'needjaunissiwauk.
Be kind to your children.

Afterwards there was a feast, and the playing of games.

The Society of Medicine

Midewewin

THE NATURE OF THE SOCIETY

The term Midewewin could mean The Society of Good Hearted Ones (from *mino* "good," and *dewewin* "hearted"). It could also mean The Resonance (from *midewe* "the sound"), as a reference to the drums and the chants that were used in its ceremonies. Of all the Ojibway societies, the Midewewin was one of the oldest.

After a long apprenticeship under the tutelage of Paemaubeet (Like Trail of Vine), an elder and a member of the Midewewin, Mishi-Waub-Kaikaik became a medicine man – as his vision had foretold. Subsequently, he was himself invited to become a member of the Midewewin. By the time Mishi-Waub-Kaikaik became a fully accredited member of the Fourth Order of the society, he was thoroughly familiar with its mythical origins, its ceremonies, and its chants. The liturgy of the Midewewin was always identical, even though the petitions and the chants themselves differed for each ceremony.

Eventually, Mishi-Waub-Kaikaik taught his knowledge of the Midewewin to other candidates for membership, as Paemaubeet had taught him.

THE ORIGIN OF THE RITUAL

In the beginning, men and women lived as long as two hundred or three hundred years, and to endure like an oak tree was attributed to the possession of powerful medicines. Then, mysteriously, the people lost the gift of health and long life.

95

One by one they caught an infection and died after a short illness. It was only a matter of time before the Anishnabeg would be wiped out.

One of the victims of this unnamed epidemic was a young boy. In the presence of the Keeper at the entrance to the Land of Souls, he trembled with sorrow. When he was asked why he grieved, the young boy replied that his people were dying, and that he wanted life for them.

Through the Keeper, Kitche Manitou granted the boy's request. The Great Spirit also revealed to the boy that the condition for entering the Land of Souls was peace of heart. The Anishnabeg were to found the Midewewin so that they could attain inner peace by seeking for the good in life, and so that they could perform rituals for the gift of good health. Because plants possessed the attributes of life, growth, and self-healing, the Anishnabeg were to seek the Musko-Cheebig (Blood Root) in the depths of the sea and bring it to land. Then Nanabush, the messenger of Kitche Manitou, would make known the proper rituals.

THE ORIGIN OF THE MEDICINE

In the beginning, men and women were happy. Surrounded by good fortune, they did not seek to harm one another. Then, one day, a man wanted to test the strength of his powers. He challenged Makataeshigun (Black Bass), the Spirit of the Underworld and the patron of night and bad dreams, to a contest – and he placed his entire family at stake.

Because it was going to be a contest for everything that he possessed, the man and his family constructed a lodge, built in accordance with custom and tradition. To invoke his powers, the man placed the image of the sparrow hawk, the swiftest of the hawks that killed other birds in flight, near the top of the lodge's central post. At the base of the post, he deposited wampum, quills, skins, medicine pouches, and rattles. Then, next to these offerings, he set a drum. Lastly, he positioned a large rock outside and to the north of his lodge.

When these preparations were complete, the man was ready. He drummed and chanted – invoking the sparrow hawk, asking it to lend its powers of flight and its striking precision to the bead that he had placed on the surface of his drum. The sparrow hawk screeched; the bead danced. And the man willed the bead into deadly flight in order to kill Makataeshigun's eldest son. What he willed happened. The bead struck Makataeshigun's son, killing him. And from this first wilful wish to inflict harm, a new principle was introduced into human existence: men could now hurt one another.

The man continued to test his powers. He placed a feather on his drum, and for the second time he chanted while he sounded the instrument. The sparrow hawk screeched, and the feather on the drum took flight. Striking Makataeshigun's eldest daughter, it killed her instantly. Taking off his bear-claw necklace, the man then placed it on the drum. Softly and gently he drummed at first; then louder and harder until the sparrow hawk screeched and the necklace danced. Flying to the underworld, the necklace encircled the throat of Makataeshigun's wife. It drew taut, gouging her flesh with its claws, until she fell.

Now the man felt strong enough to attack Makataeshigun. He sent his wampum beads to destroy his opponent, thinking to complete his triumph – but when the beads entered Makataeshigun's stomach he spat them out. Three times more the man directed the beads to kill; and each time the Spirit of the Underworld parried them. Finally, Makataeshigun cried, "Enough! Now it is my turn."

Makataeshigun constructed a lodge. He collected wampum beads and shells and pouches and skins of fishes and medicines which he assembled in the lodge next to the central post. Then he began his own ceremony.

Makataeshigun sang, asking the beings who governed the winds to carry him where he wished. And he was taken by the Keepers of the Winds, his patrons, to the upper world. There, Makataeshigun seized the man's eldest son and bore him to the underworld. After slaying the boy, he made medicine pouches out of his skin.

For a second time Makataeshigun was transported to the upper world by the forces of the wind. This time, he carried off the man's eldest daughter, and from her skin he fashioned eight medicine pouches.

In the third ritual, Makataeshigun beseeched the Keepers of

the Winds to bear the four pebbles on his drum to the upper world and to direct them against the man's wife. The woman was struck dead by the very first pebble.

By now, all the people were sickened by the killings, the abuse of medicines, and the hatred generated by the contest of powers. They sent a delegation of six spokesmen to Makataeshigun, with offerings of tobacco and wampum. The spokesmen begged the Spirit of the Underworld to stop killing, and to teach the Anishnabeg medicines instead. Listening to the spokesmen, Makataeshigun felt sorry for the people. He relented; but he reminded the delegation that it had been one of their own people who had begun the contest. It was mankind who had introduced death and hatred into the world. While Makataeshigun could teach songs and medicines – he could not restore the happiness that men had once possessed.

And so Makataeshigun gave his word that he would teach the Anishnabeg the ritual for warding off sickness and death. He would teach them chants and medicines. But, in return for his forbearance and for his knowledge, the Anishnabeg were required to invoke the name of Makataeshigun in all their ceremonies. Because the Spirit of the Underworld could not do the teaching himself, he chose the six spokesmen to perform this duty on his behalf. From now on, the six messengers were to teach their sisters and brothers, and they were never to return to their families or their homes. Not only were they not to leave the places where Makataeshigun would send them, but they were not to grant life unless the Anishnabeg first petitioned and performed the ceremony. But before sending the messengers forth into the four corners of the world, Makataeshigun assured them that with the protection of the Thunderbirds and the faith of the Anishnabeg, the medicine would endure. Not even strangers could destroy it. And Makataeshigun made an additional promise. Eventually, he said, he himself would come to the Anishnabeg in the form of a medicine.

After the messengers had left, Makataeshigun went to his adversary to offer reconciliation. The man and the Spirit of the Underworld made peace, and agreed to control the wish to hurt others. In order to accomplish this, they sought the guidance of the Autissokaunuk (Muses, or Makers of Stories), and called them to a Great Council.

The man addressed the Autissokaunuk. "Have pity on the people. Bring them peace. Keep them safe at night. Come to them in sleep. Bring them good dreams. Keep them from Makataeshigun ... he of the underworld who is the patron of bad dreams!"

"That we cannot grant," the Autissokaunuk replied. "We alone cannot consider your request; our brothers and our sisters must also be consulted. Only when all are present may we consider the matter."

The man and Makataeshigun sent a messenger to invite all the spirits of the animal and plant worlds to attend the meeting. Then the man again addressed the assembly. "Makataeshigun and I have warred now for a long time. We have inflicted a great harm upon one another and upon mankind. Still, we have made peace; and we wish to continue to live in peace.

"But Makataeshigun is the chief of the underworld and of the deep night and of sleep. It is then that he enters our world and governs us. This we cannot change – even though in the dark we are helpless against Makataeshigun. Were he to do evil, we could not defend ourselves against him.

"It is true that Makataeshigun has given his word not to harm good men and women. But we do not know how goodness may be measured. Let us know the good through dreams. Let us dream. And we shall purify ourselves to receive your words."

The Autissokaunuk and the spirits of the animal and plant worlds promised to instil good dreams in men who, through purification, aspired towards the good. And the spirits appointed the turtle as the chief bearer of good dreams and ideals from the spirit world, and the evergreen tree as the herald and symbol of knowledge.

After this, the Anishnabeg and Makataeshigun lived at peace with one another.

At length, the man who had first challenged Makataeshigun grew very old. Knowing that he would soon die, he instructed his grand-daughter to cut his corpse in a certain manner, and not to throw any portion of it away upon his death. He told her that his flesh would be transformed into an ointment, and she was to distribute this medicine to the sick. And so it came to pass.

In the underworld, Makataeshigun was also growing old. He told his grandson that when he died, his body was to be cut in a certain way so that it would become medicine. This, too, came to pass.

As time went by, the grand-daughter in the upper world had used up nearly all of her medicine. She went to the underworld in search of Makataeshigun – but instead she found the young man, Makataeshigun's grandson. Together, the two of them returned to the upper world, taking with them Makataeshigun in the form of a medicine – as had been promised to the six delegates, many years ago. It was a medicine that would protect the Anishnabeg against sickness and also bring them game.

THE SACRED SONGS

Men and women now possessed medicine and ritual. Next, they learned the mystic songs that they were to sing in all their healing ceremonies. And to communicate their feelings, the Anishnabeg were to use a drum: a wooden kettle drum with bearskin casing. This was the Midewewigun – the sacred drum.

Only the drum possessed the special tones that would be suitable for the audience of the spirits. There was no sound, human or natural, to compare to it. What the drum imparted neither man nor woman could understand, for it transcended human comprehension, going beyond it in the form of an echo that could be heard only by spirits. It was a mystery; and therefore it was the best way for man to communicate with the spirit world. While he drummed, man chanted, so that his petitions were borne by the echo of the drum and transformed into the language of the spirits who dwelled above and below and beyond. Only the talk of the drum could gain the attention of the deities.

And the Anishnabeg learned and sang many sacred chants.

SONGS OF PETITION:
> *Midewewigaewuk, ininiwuk.*
> The men make the drum echo.

> *Midewewigun, n'gaganoodumaugonaun.*
> The drum speaks for us.

> *K'geezhikoongimaunih nindowaetaun*
> *Aen-dazhi dani-tabuyaun.*
> To the skies I look and call
> Whilst I sit.

A SONG IN PETITION FOR THE DRUM:
> *Midewewigun, nindo-wiyauh.*
> I seek the drum.

A SONG IN PETITION FOR MYSTERY TO DRUM:
> *N'midewewigunim, manitouwiyauwih.*
> Upon my drum bestow the mystery.

A SONG IN PETITION TO THE SPIRITS:
> *Cheebiyuk, n'd'nindo-*
> *wauyauk.*
> I invoke the ghosts (of the departed).

A PETITION FOR HEARING:
> *N'nauneebowiyaun; n'nauneebowiyaun.*
> *Cheegi-shkwaundaeming, wauwizhigau-bowiyaun.*
> I am standing, I am standing;
> Near your doors, I will stand.

A PETITION TO ENDURE HARDSHIP:
> *Waussae/aukonae k'weeyow.*
> *K'okomissinaunih k'gah ondinimowaunaunih.*
> Bright with flame is your body.
> A mystery derived from our grandmother.

A SONG IN PETITION FOR THE PIPE (BY A WOMAN):
> *Puwaugun, nindo-wiyauh.*
> A pipe do I seek.

A SONG IN PETITION FOR MEDICINE POUCH OF FOX:
> *Waugooshaehn n'mayauwishimauh.*
> In the fox I place my trust.

SONGS TO THE HEAVENS:

> *Geezhigoong w'dah daebwaewaeshin, n'daewewigunim.*
> My drumming shall echo to the skies.

> *Aundih aen-danee/aek?*
> Where is it that you dwell?

SONGS TO THE DAWN:

> *Waubunossaedauh.*
> Let us go to the east.

> *Waubunoong gae nakawaenayaun.*
> To the east I will turn my head.

A SONG FOR LIFE:

> *Neewing ondaunimut;*
> *Neewing inaunimut.*
> From four directions blow the winds
> To four directions blow the winds.

A SONG OF THANKS FOR LIFE AND POWER:

> *Bawaudjigaeaun wae-ondji manitouwiyaun.*
> To dreams I owe the mystery.

A SONG EXPRESSING THE EXTENT OF POWER:

> *N'geewitaukummikowaeyaun.*
> Around the world I shall bear it.

A SONG FOR PRESCIENCE:

> *N'zussigodaetchigawiyaun.*
> Bad signs will I heed.

A SONG TO KNOW THE DESTINY OF A LEADER:

> *N'gah kawaedabaenimauh, ogimauh.*
> *N'gah nindo-kikaenimauh gae izhiwaebizigwaen.*
> To the test I place the chief.
> What his fate, I long to know.

A SONG FOR HELP:

> *Ayaubeetumun*
> *Naudimowik-kaetimaugozit.*
> You who abides
> Help the poor.

SONGS OF ROMANCE:
> *N'missowinowauh quae*
> *N'babaumizeekundowauh.*
> I covet the woman
> I care for the woman.

> *Shkotae-bugonee*
> *N'gah auskaugoon.*
> The flower of fire
> Will come to my aid.

A SONG FOR APPEASEMENT:
> *K'dauh bimodjiwauh w'odae/ing*
> Pierce her heart.

A SONG FOR PARDON:
> *Waegwaen apautiwaewidung, w'gauh wiyaezhimuk*
> *Tchi aubawaewaenimit, tchi aubawaewaenimit.*
> He whose voice I hear, he whom I have deceived
> Of him I seek pardon, of him I seek pardon.

A SONG FOR RECONCILIATION:
> *Maetchi-ginoonitiwaugwaen*
> *Onauminauh, n'nitawaeh.*
> On those who malign one another
> I will use my medicine.

A SONG IN MOURNING:
> *Ah! Neekauninaunih n'gee gageedawaetoonaubimin.*
> Ah! Brother, I had mourned for you.

A SONG TO THE BEAR:
> *W'dah aungishkaukawaein*
> *Anaumikummik.*
> Your footprints will fade
> As if deep into the earth.

A SONG TO DEER, MOOSE, AND CARIBOU:
> *Daeshkunidjik n'd'nindomauk.*
> I call the antlered ones.

SONGS FOR GAME:
> *Tchi manaudjimikooyaun*
> *Tchi manaudjimikooyaun, n'd'daupinumoon.*

I am honoured
I am honoured to receive your gift.

W'gawautaeshkowaun,
Kaugigae w'd'aunkaeshkowaun.
Like a shadow
Always following.

SONGS FOR GOOD HUNTING:
W'dah gaweenwipuwae.
Futile his flight.

N'gah kikinowautchitoon k'd'inaudiziwin
K'gah gagawaedabaenimin.
Your nature will I imitate
In order to test you.

K'weeyow n'gah nitton
K'cheejauk w'd'aubeetum
Onauminanbugonae n'gah gawinaeshimauh.
Your body I will kill
Your spirit will endure
I will fell him with the mystic plant.

Ayauwaunikummigauk k'gah ondjimookeewae
Auno manitouwiyin k'gah ondjimookeewae.
From the hollow of the earth you will emerge
Mystic-like you will come forth.

Gauwissaungun-weeyow maumoweenut.
Game is plentiful.

Gauwissaungunuk n'abi-izhaumikook
Kauween w'd'ningodjipuwaesseewuk.
The game came to me
The game will not run away.

Metigwaub n'nitawae
Pigook n'nitawae.
A bow will I use
An arrow will I use.

Nakwae-bimowaukun k'weekauninaun.
Unerring strike our brother.

N'd'auskaugook, kinebikowiyaunuk.
The snakes will sustain me.

Benaeswibimowaukae, onauminauh n'nitawaeh.
At birds do I aim my medicine.

N'gah kawae/auk gauwissaungnuk.
I shall stalk the game.

Migizi, migizi
N'd'izhi zheebaendum.
Nissowautikong
K'gah waubundaun zaugigun.
The eagle, the eagle
Patient like him.
From the forks on high
You will perceive a lake.

SONGS FOR GOOD FISHING:
    Wee winaunautaushimuk mishi-numae
    Mee, wee gagawaedabaenimuk.
    I shall fetch the sturgeon in the wind
    I shall test him.

    N'wauyiyaegummeegae
    N'd'aupitagummeetchigae.
    I set my nets near the shore
    I set my nets halfway across the lake.

SONGS OF THANKSGIVING:
    K'nakawaenimauko.
    We accept your gift.

    K'weeyow n'gah meedjin
    K'waeyaun n'gah beeskaun.
    Your flesh will I eat
    Your fur will I wear.

A SONG IN PLEDGE OF ACKNOWLEDGEMENT OF GIFT:
    Kikinowautchi-beegaudae.
    It shall be written.

It was in song and in drumming that the purpose and substance of ceremonies was embodied and fulfilled.

THE CEREMONIAL PROCESSION

Before beginning any ceremony, the priests and novices of the Midewewin would purify themselves. Then, they made four processions around the rectangular Midewigun, (the ceremonial lodge modelled after the one first built for the Anishnabeg by Nanabush). During the processions they rattled turtle-shell cymbals to invoke the spirits of goodwill and to repel the spirits of evil. And they chanted:

Mino-dae/aeshowishinaung
Tchi mino-inaudiziwinaungaen.
Fill our spirits with good
Upright then may be our lives.

Nanaukinumowidauh matchi-dae/aewin
Zhaugootchitumowidauh matchi-dodumowin.
Defend our hearts against evil
Against evil prevail.

The four processions that the priests and candidates made around the Midewigun were intended to symbolize the quarterly divisions existing in time, space, life, events, order, thought, and dream. There were four seasons in the year; and there were four points of the earth. There were four orders of existence and four species in the animal world and four races in man's world. There were four levels of dream; and four degrees in the operation of the mind. And there were four stages, as well as four important events, in each individual's life. As four parts, four times, occurred and recurred in the natural order – so man regulated his ceremonies into four parts: the preparation, the ceremony, the re-enactment, and the feast. By going four times around the Midewigun, the priests represented this principle in their ritual.

On their first circuit around the Midewigun, the priests and the candidates would be met by four Fourth Order Midewewin priests who were dressed in bear robes and who represented good. These four bears, joining in the chants, accompanied the procession. Further on, four more priests attired in bear skins appeared. These bears represented the forces of evil, and they snarled in mock rage and tried to stop the procession.

But the good bears swept on, pressing back the bad bears who growled and reared in feigned defiance.

THE TOTEMS

When the four circuits were completed, the men and women of the Midewewin would file into the Midewigun. Within were four posts – four trees of life – representing the four orders of the Midewewin. At the bases of the posts were the offerings of the members: gifts of tobacco, medicines, furs, implements, and birch bark scrolls; medicine pouches of bear, wolf, fox, otter, beaver, hawk, and owl. Here and there throughout the interior of the Midewigun, the carved images of the patrons of the society were set in their prescribed places. Negik (Otter), the first and leading patron, was in the centre; Noka (Bear) was both at the entrance and the exit in order to guard the ritual; and the Autissokaunuk were placed at the cardinal points. There were carvings of Moozo (Moose) and Addikmeg (Whitefish), symbolizing nourishment; as well as images of Animkee-Binaessi (Thunderbird) and Makataeshigun. Other patrons represented were Kinozhae (Pike), Numae (Sturgeon), Numaegos (Trout), Coocoocoo (Owl), Wawa (Goose), Aninzheep (Duck), Chejauk (Crane), Mong (Loon), Migizi (White Headed Eagle), Shaudae (Pelican), Amik (Beaver), Pizheu (Lynx), Waubosse (Rabbit), and Addik (Caribou).

THE SACRED SHELL

Set beside the sacred drum was the Midemegis, the sacred shell. Always present in the lodge, the shell symbolized the fact that long life was not sought for its own sake. Instead, long life was a gift that the Anishnabeg had to reclaim after it had been lost by the man who first challenged the Spirit of the Underworld.

A story was told of a band of Anishnabeg who abandoned their homes, believing that long life was to be found in the east, in the Land of Dawn that daily gave birth to the sun. They took all their possessions with them; and even though they endured untold hardships, and even though the dawn was the same distance away every morning, they continued their journey. The belief that they would eventually come to the Land of Dawn sustained and inspired them. At last they came to a great sea, greater than any lake that they had ever known, where the storms exceeded any that they had ever experienced and where the water was salt, undrinkable. And beyond this salt sea was the sunrise–the Land of Dawn, forever out of reach.

The people lingered on the shores of the great sea for a long time. But then the seashell, the Midemegis, appeared in the western sky, shining bright as a star during the day, bright as the moon during the night. The elders considered and discussed this wondrous appearance. Finally, they agreed that it was a sign for them to return to their brothers and sisters and the country they had left behind. With the Midemegis as their guide, the band retraced their journey to their homeland, where they were reunited with their tribe and restored to their traditions.

In the Weekindiwin (Ceremony of Induction), the Midemegis was used by a priest of the Fourth Order to "shoot" and "kill" a candidate, after that candidate had been successfully examined for his (or her) knowledge. Then, with his (or her) breath, the priest would revive the candidate. In this dramatic fashion was enacted life and death, loss and restoration, contagion and purification.

The Midemegis was also present in other ceremonies: Onauminauh Midewewin (Ceremony of the Medicine); Cheeby Midewewin (Ceremony of the Dead); Kinebik Midewewin (Ceremony of the Serpent); Autissokaewininiwuk Midewewin (Ceremony of the Attendants); and Gee/ossae Midewewin (Ceremony of Hunting). In all ceremonies, the sacred shell was the most essential and important element.

THE SMOKING OF THE PIPE

When everyone had filed into the lodge, a tribal Pottawae/ otomi (Keeper of the Fire), who was also a member of the society, would light a fire from the embers that he always kept alive in a special container. Kinnikinnik (a mixture of sweet grass) was used. It emitted sweet smelling fumes when it burst into flame.

From the fire, the Oshkaubaewis (Keeper of the Pipe), would light the sacred pipe. An elder of the Midewewin would then take the pipe from the keeper, and hold it reverently as he made an invocation.

"Great Mystery! Look upon our thoughts and upon our ritual. We ask you to look with favour upon our ceremony and upon our deeds. We need your guidance and your favour so that we may do what is good.

"Mother Earth! We honour you as we honour our mothers. We thank you for all the benefits that you have bestowed upon us. You have given us plants for food and medicine. You have given us beauty to behold. You are the first of mothers. You are mother to all mankind."

And, on behalf of the Anishnabeg, the elder would make his petitions.

PETITION TO THE NORTH

To you, muses, who dwell and abide to the north: this day we ask you to grant us good dreams. Come this night and every night. Come into our homes and into our minds and fill us with the yearning for good. Show us the good that we may follow and observe it.

Banish evil dreams from our sleep and from our lives. Let neither deceit nor remorse, neither selfishness nor ill will towards our brothers, disturb our sleep.

Guard us at night when we are helpless. Come like the north winds; dispel the evil. Watch over us, blanket our spirits as the snow covers the earth. And do not abandon us until we are awake and restored.

PETITION TO THE WEST

To you, muses, who dwell and abide to the west: bestow upon us goodwill. Show us the path so that we do not stumble or stray. Inspire us with goodwill so that we may achieve. Teach us to seek after kindness, courage, cheerfulness, wisdom, patience, and fairness. And give us the wisdom to know right from wrong.

Let me not think ill of my brothers or my sisters. Let me not doubt our forefathers' teachings, or despise the animals of the forest, or forget the poor, or scorn our ceremonies, or envy my brothers and sisters, or distrust my vision, or cower when in danger.

Let us seek goodwill. Help us honour the Great Mystery, our forefathers, our parents, and our dead. Inspire us when we are in doubt and in sorrow; lend us strength when we are in danger and when we falter. Temper our anger and envy. Endow us with forbearance. And guide us in abiding by our visions.

PETITION TO THE SOUTH

We were given speech by the Great Spirit to foster goodwill among ourselves, and to commune with the spirits. It has both a practical and a spiritual end. It is a sacred act.

But we have too often given hurt by angry words, or misled our brothers and sisters by hasty words. When giving council, we have offered the benefit of our experience and knowledge either too soon or too late to do good. By habit, we either talk too much or too little. And we have often paid heed to untruths about our neighbours, and then carried them abroad.

If we utter words as if they are nothing more than sound, our thoughts will be regarded as shallow and worthless ... and so will we. And if we are careless of the truth we must, in the end, lose the trust of our brothers and sisters.

In order to inspire trust we must attend to our elders, who have urged us to listen and to talk – but to be as gentle in our speech as the balm of the south wind.

PETITION TO THE EAST

When we wake at dawn we are refreshed and ready to direct our hands and our feet to our labour. But we also remember that among us are brothers and sisters who cannot look forward to the new day with the same spirit as ourselves. With us dwell a blind man, a lame woman, several orphans, a widow, a mute, and a woman seeking dream.

Our patron! With our hearts, our arrows, and our medicines, we will make the day as light as we can for our brothers and sisters. We will lead the blind man, we will bear the lame woman, we will shelter the orphans, we will comfort the widow, we will speak for the mute, and we will guide the woman seeking dream.

Make game abundant, corn plentiful, and medicines strong for them and for us.

PETITION TO MAKATAESHIGUN

Finally, the elder would make an appeal to Makataeshigun, the Spirit of the Underworld. This was the remembrance that Makataeshigun had requested, when he first gave medicines to the people:

Patron of the deep
Patron of the dark
Patron of the night
Patron of the arcane
Patron of the hidden.
Forbear!
Stay far
From our sleep
From our minds
From our hearts
From our spirits.
Let our spirits wander
From depth to depth
From breadth to breadth,
Inward and outward
Within their beings,
In quest for peace.

THE END OF THE CEREMONY

After the petitions had been finished, there would always be utter stillness within the Midewigun. The only motion would be that of the fire, thrusting towards infinity. The only sound would be that of the flames, crackling in the quiet. In search of good, the priests had withdrawn into the very depths of themselves. And there, within, the priests and the candidates were to achieve the final state of contemplation.

It was in this state that good was to be found; but it was in the present, in the world of man, that it was to be used. And the reward for good was long life–so that the elders could teach the good and exemplify it and pass it on to the younger generation.

Later, the kettle drum would be uncased, and the principal chants that had been taught to the Anishnabeg would be sung. The beat of the drum bore the petitions from the present to the beyond, and to the patrons of good. If the petitioners were purified and had faithfully observed the ritual in all its particulars, the Autissokaunuk heard the drumming and the chanting. They would deliver the petitions above and below: above to Kitche Manitou, and below to the Makataeshigun.

When an answer was obtained, the ceremony would finally draw to a close; and the society would feast and dance in thanksgiving.

The Society of the Dawn

Waubunowin

THE ORIGIN OF THE SOCIETY

It was said that the Waubunowin was dedicated to the practice of sorcery, and that its members were inspired by evil. No one was quite sure.

The uncertainty bred many rumours. Some said that the society had been formed long ago by members of the Third Order of the Midewewin who had refused to abide by the Midewewin's code. Since they were thus believed to support evil, these members were outcast; and they then formed their own society. Others said that the society had its origins in sorcerers who had once intimidated the Anishnabeg. Still others pointed out that since the term "waubunoh" meant dawn, the society might have been borrowed from an eastern tribe, one of the Waubunakaek – or that it might have had its beginnings in Moningwunaekauning (Place of the Yellow Woodpecker), when a wandering band of Anishnabeg returned from their unsuccessful search for the Land of Dawn. Then again, the name might only refer to the society's practice of conducting its rituals during the night and concluding them at dawn.

One thing that was constant was the people's fear of the Waubunowin. The power of the society was no less than that exercised by the Third Order of the Midewewin; but while a member of the Midewewin sought to invoke the spirits of good and to perform good deeds, the members of the Waubunowin were reputed to summon the spirits of evil, and to use conjuring to inflict harm on others. People seldom spoke of the

Waubunowin; and when they did, they did so with respect.

Mishi-Waub-Kaikaik did not believe that the Waubunowin was entirely dedicated to committing evil. Except for one ceremony, all the society's rituals were performed in seclusion and under the cover of night; and Mishi-Waub-Kaikaik believed that it was this mystery which made the Waubunowin seem sinister. Since he was a member of the Midewewin, Mishi-Waub-Kaikaik could not join the Waubunowin. But, like the rest of the community, he participated yearly in the public portion of the Ceremony in Petition for Life and Health.

PREPARATION

Once again, winter was approaching the land. The bright hues drained from any leaves that still clung to the trees. The forests were silent except for the flutter and call of chickadees. And more and more frequently the wind drove from the north, lashing lakes and pushing clouds before it.

It was time for the Waubunowin to convene for their final ceremony. Before the families that made up the village withdrew to their separate wintering territories, the Waubunowin would conduct, in private and in public, their autumn ceremony: the Ceremony in Petition for Life and Health. Not until spring would the families come together once more. Not until spring would the Waubunowin meet again.

For Tikumiwaewidung (He Whose Voice Echoes Across the Lake), this performance of the ceremony was special. He had been recently initiated into the society, and the occasion would mark the first time that he would officiate as a fully accredited member. This time, too, there was an additional purpose to the ritual. An old woman of the tribe was sick, drained of strength and breath by the years. It was incumbent upon the society to try to restore her to health.

Everyone was busy. The hunters scoured the forests for deer and moose, and young boys flushed out rabbits and partridges. The women began to prepare the grand feast, while the girls gathered wood for the fire. Members of the society prepared medicines, collected tobacco, and assembled gifts. They also constructed the lodges that were needed for the ceremony.

116

THE MAIN LODGE

The sacred lodge was erected first. Circular in shape, it represented the circumference of the earth and sky, and reflected the timelessness of space. It had two entrances: one facing the west and the other facing the east. The saplings that made up its walls were arched, so that they would have formed a dome if they had been joined. But the lodge was not meant to be completely enclosed. Instead, at the height of about twelve feet, there was a large opening. It allowed a tall centre post to extend freely upward; and it admitted the light of the sun and the stars.

When the walls of the lodge were completed, the old men and women who were the most senior members of the Waubunowin brought in their offerings. Wampum shells, tobacco, and clothing were assembled near the central post. Then, with deliberate reverence, the guardians of the images unfolded the buckskin casings that enveloped each carving of the society's patrons, and placed the images in their prescribed places. Shawaegeezhig (Sloping Sky) was placed in the middle, next to the central post. Misquogeezhig (Red Sky), the east; Kababonkaugeezhig (Winter Sky), the north; Minoonigeezhig (Pleasing Sky), the west; and Zhawanogeezhig (Blue Sky), the south – were set on pedestals at the cardinal points within the lodge. Other statuettes of patrons and totems were brought in and set down. And lastly, a pallet for the sick old woman was constructed near the central post.

THE PURIFICATION LODGES

While the more elderly men and women were adorning the main lodge, another group, under the guidance and supervision of an elder, was busy constructing purification lodges. Four of these were built in a straight line from the eastern entrance of the main lodge; and another four were built in a straight line from the western entrance. From one purification lodge to another, the celebrants and other participants would pass, purifying themselves before entering the main structure.

Tikumiwaewidung, because he was to perform the Pipe of Peace Ceremony, would be the first to undergo purification.

117

Even though he had endured many purifications, each one was an ordeal, always difficult. It was to be pushed to the limits of endurance without giving in: to overcome hunger and thirst, to withstand the demands of the flesh for relief, and to vanquish pain. It was to go beyond this state to the next: to surmount lust and selfishness and doubt, to subdue the ravages of the passions and, finally, to attain that state of being free from the clamour of the body and the turmoil of the mind. When all these things were done, Tikumiwaewidung would be deemed worthy to address Kitche Manitou and all the other spirits in the course of conducting the ceremony.

One by one, the other members of the Waubunowin would go through the same rites until the entire membership was purified. Only then, when they were all cleansed, could they commune with the spirits.

THE PIPE OF PEACE

Since he was the first to be purified, Tikumiwaewidung was the first to enter the sacred lodge for the beginning of the ceremony. He was wearing his ceremonial dress, and he sat deep in thought while the others arrived. He did not look up as they took their places. He was considering what he was about to say.

No words were uttered by anyone. And none were needed. The silence, solemn and deep, was an extension of the Great Peace. It was to be preserved, undisturbed by sound, for as long as possible.

In the stillness within the lodge, the Pipe Bearer unbound the sacred pipe from its buckskin casing and set it on a blanket. Handling both the pipe and the tobacco pouch with deep veneration, he filled the pipe and lit it. Then he handed the pipe to Tikumiwaewidung.

Tikumiwaewidung blew a puff of smoke towards the sky that could be seen through the top of the lodge. "Great Spirit!" he said. "We honour you this day, and we thank you for life and for all things. Accept this, our poor offering. It is all that we have; but this tobacco is your gift to us, and now we humbly offer you your gift in the form of smoke. We have cleansed our hearts and beings to be worthy of addressing you. You have been kind. Have pity on us now. Accept this smoke –our offering to you."

He blew a second puff of smoke, this time in honour of the earth. "Mother Earth!" he said. "We honour you this day, and we thank you for life and for all things. You are our mother. You feed us, you clothe us, you shelter us, and you comfort us. For this we thank you and honour you."

And Tikumiwaewidung went on to appeal to the north, the south, the east, and the west; offering to each a puff of smoke from the pipe. His appeal was for the people, and for the sick woman who lay on her pallet near the central pole.

PETITION TO THE NORTH

To you who reside and abide to the north: we offer you our gratitude and we honour you. Temper your winds, your snows, and your storms so that we may survive, so that our children may not get sick, and so that our elders may not suffer. We come to you for guidance. Help us to remember that if we are not wise, and if we neglect the future, we shall bear the consequences. Assist us in making wise decisions.

Remember us and have compassion upon us when you come to test us –when you strip the trees of life; when you send the fish into the deep; when you drive the animals from their haunts. Be kind to our older brothers the moose, the deer, the bear, the beaver, and the squirrel. Keep them well and safe, for they, too, must live. And for our sister's sake, temper your spirit and your breath.

Come not too quickly or too soon. Be not harsh. Stay not too long.

PETITION TO THE SOUTH

To you who reside and abide to the south: we offer you our gratitude and we honour you. If this summer past we have eaten well, travelled far, and seen our brothers and sisters –if our eyes have beheld the colours and the forms of Mother Earth and our ears have heard chantings in the forest –if we have reaped medicines and harvested meat and fish and corn, it is because of your generosity. If we do not hunger and if we do not suffer hardship this coming winter, we owe our good fortune to you.

We come to you for guidance. As you have been kind to us, let us not be any less kind to our brothers and sisters and strangers, in spirit and in deed. Let us bear the young and the old, the living and the dead, the well and the sick in our hearts. As you have nourished us, so let us feed the weak, the lame, and the sick; the widows and the orphans. Remind us to be strong. Sustain us in our resolve.

Have compassion on us; do not allow us to forget. Warm our hearts as you warm Mother Earth, so that our thoughts may grow into good deeds just as the seed grows into corn. And should we falter, overlook our weakness.

And have pity on our sister. Heal her pains as you melt the snows and ice, and as you warm the waters. Spare her. Allow her to see more summers, more grandchildren.

Do not stay away too long. Do not forget us. Come back soon.

PETITION TO THE EAST

To you who reside and abide to the east: we offer you our gratitude and we honour you. With your coming you regenerate all things from sleep; you bring all things from half-death with your light. You awaken the birds who praise you with song. You awaken the flowers who unfold their petals. You awaken the squirrel and the chipmunk to play. You awaken us refreshed and renewed to face a new day; and you awaken the children with increased strength for greater good. You make light that which was dark. You restore us from the realm of half-death to the world of the living.

As you illuminate the world for us, let us enlighten our children so that they can see their way clearly. Permit us to pass to them the wisdom bestowed upon us by our ancestors, so that the young, too, may grow strong and wise and kind and brave. May they awaken from good dreams to do good deeds.

Let us therefore remember the young in our deliberations.

They look to us for guidance, as we look to them with hope. That is our gift to them. May they cherish that gift and enlarge it.

And have pity on our sister. As you awakened us from sleep, restore her to health from sickness. She has much good to impart.

Let us do good today, and the day after that, and the next.

PETITION TO THE WEST

To you who reside and abide to the west: we offer you our gratitude and we honour you. Each day you remind us of life: with the sun's rise, birth and youth; with the sun's set, old age and death. You remind us by the swiftness of the day how short life is. To see the sunrise and behold the sunset is a joy. To know life from its youth to its old age is a gift. You remind us of our destiny.

When your skies glow, we know that your light will soon be gone. Even the birds know that your light will dim, and they lament. Flowers fold their petals, and the squirrels and chipmunks go to their nests. We, tired from our work, go to our rest. But we know that light will return .... Not so with life. No matter how much we may wish it to linger, we cannot hold back one day. And no matter how much we may wish to prolong our lives, we cannot hold back death. Like the day, so will men and women grow weak and die and proceed to the Land of Souls, where they will be united with their forbears. As your skies glow brightly just before sunset, may we, too, give light to our children. May our good deeds shine as brightly as the sun; and may we go to the Land of Souls with peace in our hearts.

And have compassion on our sister. Keep her well this night, and let her see the rise of another sun without suffering.

May we sleep this night in the peace that you bring. May we have good dreams; and may we fulfil them on the morrow. Let us be true.

CLOSING THE PETITION

After he had finished the individual appeals to the north, the south, the east, and the west, Tikumiwaewidung went on to address all of these deities together. He asked for sustenance during the coming winter, so that the Waubunowin could again meet for celebration when the snows were gone. He thanked the Great Mystery for the gift of healing, and for the knowledge of the mystic rituals that could be performed for the good of the sick.

Next, Tikumiwaewidung addressed each of the images of totems and patrons that were set throughout the lodge. He began with the otter, who had once saved the Anishnabeg from extinction by bringing a healing plant from the depths of the waters, and who had been elected the patron of the society and the symbol of healing. Then Tikumiwaewidung went on to the other images, recounting what each represented, and what it meant to the tribe. He only stopped speaking after he had acknowledged how much the people were indebted to the bear, the moose, the whitefish, the pike, the sturgeon, and all the rest of the animals. His opening petition had taken up the greater part of the morning.

Now, silence again settled into the lodge. All the celebrants withdrew into their own souls, attempting to pass, from there, into the realm of the spirits. Finally, two old men and an old woman rose from their places. They took up three drums that lay at the base of the central pole, initiating the next phase in the ceremony.

THE RITUAL FOR LONG LIFE

Softly, the drums beat in unison. In a high-pitched voice, using an ancient language remembered only by a few, the woman began to chant. After her, the second and third chanters sang in their turn. Each chanter made an entreaty to the spirits and the mysteries.

Tibishko zhingwauk n'gah inaudiss.
Like the pine would I be.

Tibishko assin n'gah aubeetum.
Like the rock would I abide.

Tibishko nibi n'gah danee.
Like the water would I stay.

Then three more celebrants got up; and they, too, chanted in turn.

Gautawaenimishinaung tchi aukozissiwaung.
Keep us from sickness.

K'mashki-akeemewauh manitouwun.
Your medicines are potent.

Gaunaundiziwin minowaunigowaendaugot.
Good health is blessed.

The sequence continued, with priests getting up to make their petitions in groups of three, until all the celebrants had performed. And then – a remarkable thing happened. Even before the last trio of celebrants finished chanting, there was a rush of wind. It was faint at first, and as gentle as a breeze of spring; and then it increased in force until it was like a whirlwind, overpowering every other sound. At the same time, all of the carved images began to tremble in their places, as if they danced to the beat of the wind. And above the tumult rose the chants of the supernatural beings, thin and frail, yet clearly penetrating the wind's thunderous voice. All the men and women within the lodge gave themselves completely and utterly to the choir until it, and the wind, faded away. The spirits had answered.

As if inspired by the passing of the spirits, two priests bearing blow-guns rose to their feet. They began to dance around the old woman lying on her pallet; and as they danced, they discharged missiles of small shells at a bird skin lying near her on the ground. All about them, the other celebrants chanted, "Bemaudizih! Bemaudizih! Bemaudizih!" (Life! Life! Life!) And another remarkable thing occurred. Under the falling shells the bird skin came to life, regenerated by an act whose function was to kill. Chanting triumphantly, the two priests released the bird into the sky.

Then, still chanting, the priests washed their hands in a bowl of water. They knelt in front of the fire, their cleansed hands wet and dripping, and their chant changed. "N'dah shkotaewimim! N'd'autaetomim shkotae!" (We are of the fire! We put out the fire!) Leaning forward, they scooped up coals with their bare fingers; and with their extended hands cupping mounds of fiery embers, they began to dance around the lodge. They sang, "N'pottowae/otomeemim!" (We are the keepers of the fire!) And they continued to dance until the coals grew dim and cold and were reduced to ash.

THE RITUAL OF THANKSGIVING

It was already well on in the afternoon, the air chill, when Tikumiwaewidung finally rose from his place. He took a procession of priests and candidates outside the lodge, leading it to the outskirts of the village where he stopped to plant a kernel of corn. This was the part of the ceremony that the entire village witnessed. Tikumiwaewidung said:

Manitouwih meenkaunaehnse.
Neegiwin manitouwun.
Meenkaunaehnse w'dah kikinowauzinowaun abinoodjeehn.
Meenkaunaehnse manitouwih, w'dah mashki-akeewih.
The seed is a mystery.
Growth is a mystery.
The seed symbolizes a child.
The seed is mystical, it will heal.

Afterwards, everyone feasted. They ate venison, beaver, moose, and muskrat; whitefish, trout, and pike; partridge, duck, and goose; corn and dried fruit. The feast was significant. Not only did it represent the skills of both the hunters and the women, but it betokened a good winter. Throughout the feast, the villagers talked of the past summer's harvest of fruit and fish, and of the herds of deer and moose that were now in the forests. They spoke of the signs that the coming winter would be mild. It was a happy occasion.

Later, while men and women smoked, the young boys and girls collected even more wood for the grand fire. When they had gathered enough, a great blaze was kindled, and the drummers brought out a large drum that they adjusted and re-adjusted until it was taut and resonant.

At the first beat of the drum and the first swell of chant from the drummers, all the men and women got up to form a great dance circle about the central fire. As the flames crackled and curled and licked the air, the dancers moved around them. The women's movements were gently weaving, the men's movements vigorous; but all danced in rhythm with the beat of the drum. It was a beat that corresponded with the heartbeat of life; and the dance did not stop until the drummers themselves brought the Ritual of Thanksgiving to a close.

Then it was time for the young to succeed their elders in the dance – as they would succeed them in life. The young boys and girls danced in a lighter, less solemn mood. They danced to please; they danced to elicit laughter. Often they did evoke laughter with their spontaneous performances, as they caricatured the habits of animals and humans. As the afternoon gradually drew to a close, the dancers performed The Close Your Eyes Dance, The Prairie Chicken Dance, The Dragonfly Dance, The Frog Mating Dance, The Swallow Hunger-Flight Dance, The Robin Envy Dance, and many other dances whose sole purpose was to amuse. It was not until the creeping grey shadows enveloped the camp that the dancing and the celebration came to an end.

THE FINAL VIGIL

But the day was not yet over for the members of the Waubunowin. Once more, the society gathered together in the sacred lodge, ready for the last part of a ceremony that would end only at dawn.

When everyone was seated, the tribal storyteller was invited to recount the story of the people. He spoke of the beginning of all things in the vision of the Great Mystery; and of the mystic origins of the Anishnabeg. He spoke of the four Spirit Beings who were sent to help the people; and of the five Water Beings who tested the people for their kindness, and then gave them the reward of knowledge. He told his listeners of how the Anishnabeg established settlements across the land; and of how one band, travelling far in search of the Land of Dawn, was led back home by the sacred shell.

From the history of the people, the storyteller turned to the origin and nature of their beliefs and customs and rituals. When he had come to the end of his account, he said: "All things began with vision. All things have their origin in vision. But nothing can exist without fulfilment. Whatever is, whatever comes into existence, whatever is generated or created – everything is the product of deed and performance. Even vision is brought into being. So we, too, must seek vision and dream and live out our dreams ...."

It was very late when the storyteller had finished. Outside it was black and cold. The time had come to consider life itself. Now the elders, the most senior members of the Waubunowin who had lived longest and understood life best, would instruct those who were younger.

There were eight advisers altogether: four old men and four old women who, because they had either witnessed or endured many forms of human suffering and triumph, were believed to be endowed with the virtues of wisdom and patience. They possessed something that was rare, something that all the members of the society wished to acquire. They had long life, the mystery of living on – a gift from the Great Mystery for surmounting many trials. Experience and survival gave the elders credibility, sanctioning their speech. And so they would teach, not by moralizing or by admonishing but by telling stories, using the words in which they themselves had first been instructed. The stories held their own truths; and the listeners would draw meaning from them as their hearts and minds allowed. To guide was to encourage and to point the way. As it was said: *Watch the sunset; it will foretell the morrow.*

In truth, there was only one story. It was the story of life, known as The Path of Life, within which there were many episodes. It was of this path that Tikumiwaewidung spoke when, as the principal celebrant, he introduced the elders.

"Life," said Tikumiwaewidung, "is like a seed. It begins within the earth, small and unseen and unheard; but it is there. Not until time has elapsed, not until it is ready, does it emerge. Not until spring, when the snows are gone and the sun is warm, does it come forth. And when it does appear, it grows into a plant fed by the earth, warmed by the sun, and watered by the rain. Seed becomes plant. It is a mystery.

"Human life is like a kernel of corn. The kernel does not beget itself. It must be planted and watered. And when it bursts forth, it must be cared for until it is ready to bear fruit.

So it is with a child. A child must be fed and clothed and sheltered until it can do all these things for itself. And just as the kernel of corn must be planted in good soil, so a child must be shown a path that he is to follow.

"Each person has a path to follow that our elders called The Path of Life. It winds and twists, ascends and descends, travelling over four steep hills. Along the course are traps: Weendigoes, Great Serpents, walls of fire, sweet-voiced mermaids, taunting warriors, crimson swans, good lodges, and rich hunting grounds. The stories we will hear tonight are about men and women who resisted these traps, and who kept to their path as revealed in vision. They trembled in the presence of Weendigoes, but were not overcome; they dreaded the Great Serpents, but slew them. They faltered before the fire, but passed through it; they were enticed by the mermaids, but did not turn aside. They withstood ridicule without taking revenge; they saw marvels without flinching. And although they were tempted by comfort and by plenty, they persevered in their journey. Such men and women have been granted long life.

"Now ... let us listen to our elders."

One after another the eight advisers told stories illustrating all that was worthy of praise in human conduct. And by the time they had finished their tales, dawn was beginning to lighten the sky. Tikumiwaewidung, who had connected the elders' accounts with his own remarks as befitted the principal celebrant, now spoke to bring the ceremony to an end.

"Life began with vision," Tikumiwaewidung said. "The Great Mystery saw. The Great Mystery created. And what the Great Mystery created, he will one day end. Our elders say that once again, as in the days before the Anishnabeg came to be, waters will cover the earth. On that day, all things will come to an end.

"Great Mystery! Show us the way; tell us the way. Although we may stumble, we will regain our balance. And if we do, finally, all that is right – grant us long life and peace of heart."

And then Tikumiwaewidung turned towards the pallet where the old woman lay. He told her that even if she were to die there was no need for her to be afraid. Her death would be the wish of Kitche Manitou, and she would be journeying to join her parents and all those who loved her. In the Land of Souls she would find eternal summer and eternal happiness, for in that land there was no hardship or pain or sorrow. A feast and a great celebration awaited her arrival.

But ... there was a way to discover whether she was going to die or not. Before a spirit got to the Land of Souls, it had to travel along the Path of Souls. The spirits of those who came near death could approach that path – but if they were driven away from it by the hisses of those who had truly died, then it was said that death did not yet await them.

Tikumiwaewidung asked the old woman if, during the ceremony, she had heard the hissing of the spirits. After a moment, she nodded; and Tikumiwaewidung raised his hands.

"That is good!" he said. "Those who have heard the spirits have lived long. We are glad. Your family will be glad. Sleep now. And rest." He turned to look at the rest of the gathering. "It is time to go .... Until we meet again."

And the Society of the Dawn filed out of the sacred lodge.

As Tikumiwaewidung had said, the old woman recovered; and she lived for ten more years. She had seen the Path of Souls – but more importantly, she had heard the spirits send her away. She possessed something more powerful than medicine: the gift of life that could take her from the Land of the Living to the Path of Souls and back again. To the end of her days the people brought their sick to her, to receive the benefits of her touch.

The Ritual of the Dead

Pagidaendijigewin

DEATH OF A WARRIOR

Zhawaeshk (Dagger) was dead. He had been a renowned warrior in Mishi-Waub-Kaikaik's village; but on his last War Path he had been badly wounded. Even if he had recovered, he would have been a cripple for the rest of his life; and so, when they heard of his death, the people nodded among themselves. "It is a good thing," they said. "Zhawaeshk was too proud a warrior to depend on others for the rest of his days. Now his suffering is over. It is a good thing."

But it was not a good thing for Zhawaeshk's family. It was sad to see Zhauwoonoquae (Woman of the South), his wife, bent over in sorrow, and to hear her wail for her companion-in-life. It was sad to see his sons regarding their father with bewildered looks, and to hear his daughters keen. Zhawaeshk had died with dignity. But now his family was alone.

THE ORIGIN OF BURIAL DRESS

Two women of the tribe came to prepare the corpse. They washed Zhawaeshk's body and braided his hair and dressed him in his warrior's clothing. They gathered his possessions: his weapons and pipe; his tobacco, flints, and tinder; a blanket; a small birch bark container; a wooden bowl and a wooden spoon. Zhawaeshk was gone on a long journey. He would need his personal possessions as he travelled from this life to the Land of Souls along the Path of Souls. When he finally reached his destination he would be ready for the recep-

131

tion and the Festival of Souls that was to be held in his honour.

Zhawaeshk had been a warrior. As a warrior he had died, as a warrior he would enter the Land of Souls, and as a warrior he would abide with his people and with his kind. It was fitting, then, to dress Zhawaeshk in his warrior's clothing – following the custom that had been established long ago.

Once, a woman fell into an intense fever, becoming so ill that those attending her thought that she was dead. Leaving her body in this world, the woman's spirit walked along the Path of Souls. She walked until she came to a hill that sloped down to a river. Here she was detained by an old man, the Keeper at the entrance to the Land of Souls.

"Those who enter here must be properly attired," the old man told the woman. "If they are not, they will not be admitted. Watch!"

The woman saw a procession of spirits and she watched them, observing their manner of dress. From time to time the Keeper drew her attention to one or another of the spirits.

"There!" said the Keeper. "That is the way medicine men and women are to be dressed." He pointed to a dancing woman whose hair was braided. On both her cheeks was a brown spot crossed by a horizontal bar of brilliant crimson. Over her left arm hung her medicine bag. All her garments – moccasins, cape, and robe – were brown with red bars. Even her personal possessions were brown: her bowl, spoon, sewing accessories, cooking utensils, and blanket. Behind the dancing medicine woman was a medicine man. He was wearing his finest garments; and he carried a pipe, tobacco, flint, tinder, a small cooking vessel, a dish, and a spoon. His clothes were also of the richest brown.

"There!" the Keeper said again. "He, too, must show who he was." This time he pointed to a warrior, who was re-enacting his triumphs in dance. The plumes of his head-dress waved and the shells on his anklets tinkled as he recited his exploits. In his hand he bore his war club; and from a belt around his waist hung his bag of provisions and personal possessions – everything that he needed.

Beside the warrior was a child, running sometimes, sometimes stopping to examine a butterfly, pursuing his own path at his own carefree pace. He wore a loin cloth, leggings, and a coat, while on his feet were a pair of moccasins. His hair was neatly braided; and he carried a small bow and arrow, a little dish, and a small spoon. Whenever he sat down, he played with a bone and ring game, and a plum stone game.

"Why does the child have holes in the soles of his moccasins?" the woman asked.

"Children who walk and run wear holes in their moccasins," the Keeper explained. "Only those unable to walk have moccasins without holes. It is the nature and destiny of children to run and play—it is far better for them to move than to lie helpless. If they arrive in the Land of Souls helpless, helpless they will be. But if they arrive here able to walk and run, then they will play—and they will wear holes in their moccasins."

Finally, the woman left the Keeper, and her spirit returned to her own body. When she recovered from her fever she related her vision to the people. And from then on, the people dressed their dead in the ways that the woman had seen in the Land of Souls.

PREPARATION FOR THE FIRST INSTRUCTION

At last, the two attending women were finished with their task. Zhawaeshk lay on a pallet, dressed in his ceremonial head-dress and his chest shield, his face painted in the way he used to paint it whenever he had gone on the War Path. Beside him were his weapons and his personal possessions. Bending down, one of the women cut off a lock of Zhawaeshk's hair. Wrapping it in a birch bark packet, she gave it to Zhauwoonoquae.

Then Mishi-Waub-Kaikaik, in his role as a Fourth Order member of the Midewewin, arrived to conduct the burial ceremonies. He sat next to the body, on the side where Zhawaeshk's father, mother, and brothers and sisters were also sitting. On the other side of the pallet sat Zhauwoonoquae and her children. Mishi-Waub-Kaikaik chanted:

K'neekaunissinaun, k'd'ninguzhimim.
Our brother, you leave us.

133

K'neekaunissinaun, k'maudjauh.
Our brother, you are leaving.

K'neekaunissinaun, k'cheeby/im.
Our brother, your spirit.

K'neekaunissinaun, neewi-goon cheeby-meekunnuh.
Our brother, four days on the Path of Souls.

K'neekaunissinaun, waukweeng k'd'izhau.
Our brother, to the Land of Souls you are bound.

Mishi-Waub-Kaikaik paused. When he spoke again he would be addressing the soul/spirit of Zhawaeshk. It was there: unseen, but seeing; unheard, but hearing; unsensed, but sensing. Sundered from its physical form, it lingered near its body, slowly taking leave while the transformation from chee-jauk (soul/spirit) to cheeby (spirit) took place. It was said that four days were required before the transformation was complete and the spirit was fit to enter its new life. Four days were needed for the soul/spirit to travel the space from the Land of the Living to the Land of Souls.

Mishi-Waub-Kaikaik began to speak.

THE PATH OF LIFE

Our ancestors taught us – and the Midewewin teaches us – that there is a Land of Souls. In that land there is no sickness, no hunger, no sorrow, no anger, and no envy. It is a Land of Peace inhabited by men and women of peace. For them there is plenty and comfort and joy.

Our ancestors tell us that only men and women of peace may enter there. Others will suffer hardship and misfortune and sickness in this life. Or they will be caught in the river that divides the Land of the Living from the Land of Souls.

The Midewewin tells us that we must lead good lives – following the Path of Life. The Path of Life will give us good fortune, good health, and peace of heart in this world; and bring us admission into the Land of Souls.

And the Midewewin tells us what the Path of Life is.

We must honour Kitche Manitou and thank him for life – for the winds, the sun, the waters, and the land we live on.

We must honour our elders – for they are the recipients of a great gift of long life from Kitche Manitou. If they are slow and feeble and sometimes infirm, we must feed them, help them, listen to them, and be patient. That is also our destiny. Someday we, too, will be old.

We must honour our elder brothers – the wolf and the bear, the eagle and the robin, the snake and the turtle, the butterfly and the snail, the whitefish and the trout. We must honour the rose and the corn. On them we depend for food and clothing. Treat them well, so that when you want them they will allow you to take them. You will never need. They will look after you.

We must honour women – our grandmothers and mothers, our wives and our sisters, and all the others. Treat your wife with kindness. She is your companion and friend on the Path of Life. Look after her and she will look after you. Comfort her, cheer her, speak well of her and all her sisters.

We must keep our promises and uphold our pledges. If we undertake to do something for another, we must fulfil our word by deed – otherwise we are false. If we receive a vision we must live out the vision – otherwise we are untrue. Without truth to self and to others there is no trust.

We are to be kind to everyone. Children listening to their parents: that is kindness. Parents teaching their children: that is kindness. A hunter giving meat to the elderly or to the widowed: that is kindness. A medicine man or woman healing the sick: that is kindness. A woman feeding a stranger: that is kindness. A man sheltering a stranger: that is kindness. Do something for your people. Use your gifts and your dreams for good.

We are to be peaceful. Dark dreams beget more dark dreams, and cause clouded, troubled thoughts. Twisted thoughts stir up violent passions; boiling passions give rise to burning words; and fiery speech breeds hurts and bad deeds. Seek good dreams. Temper your thoughts, your passions, your words, and your deeds. All this is hard to achieve. But we must strive for peace of heart in this life and peace of soul in the next.

We are to be courageous. The more you know, the more you trust, and the less you fear. We see this in children. A boy will start in fright when he first hears a wolf howl at night. His

135

grandmother tells him: "It is only a wolf. He is talking, listen to him. Someday you will understand the wolf." And the child's fear subsides because he begins to understand, and because he trusts his grandmother. A girl will recoil in fear when she first sees a snake. Her mother tells her: "The snake means no harm. She is out foraging for food for her little ones." And the child loses her fear of the snake when she learns something of its nature .... If you are at peace and remember that your totem and patron watch over you, you will be courageous.

Lastly, we are to be moderate in our dreams, thoughts, words, and deeds. We are never to indulge too much in one thing at the expense of another. Do not play too much; do not sleep too long. Do not eat too much; do not talk too often. Listen and watch. Someday you will be wise.

THE ORIGIN OF BURIAL RITES

After he had finished this first part of the ceremony, Mishi-Waub-Kaikaik departed. He would return later, to give the second instruction. A small party of men also left the gathering, going to a nearby grove to dig a grave. The immediate family and the women of the village remained by the body in watch, keening and wailing. Zhawaeshk's wife and mother stroked his hair and forehead, and caressed his hands to comfort him.

It was said by the old people that a man's soul/spirit could exist on four different planes or levels. On the first plane it gave life and motion to a body, and was itself sentient and conscious. On the second plane – when, for instance, the body was in sleep – the soul stayed in the body while the spirit roamed: travelling through space and time, moving through the past, the present, and the future, awakening the body on its return. On the third plane, the spirit left the body to take up sentient existence in another dimension. This happened when the body was badly injured by blow or fire or disease. The fourth and final plane was existence in the Land of Souls.

At this moment, Zhawaeshk was still on the third plane. A story was told of Beedut (Coming Storm), who had been to that plane, and who had returned with instructions about the way in which the people should bury their dead.

Beedut assembled a war party of eight warriors. Although the medicine man warned against the enterprise, Beedut insisted on leading his men into the country of the Dakota. He wished to gain honours by ambushing some of the enemy warriors.

In a forest not far from a village of the Dakota, Beedut concealed his war party among the thick pines and cedars. Then he sent out three warriors as decoys to lure the Dakota into ambush. Soon, as Beedut had expected, the Dakota pursued the decoys directly into the trap. There were twelve of the enemy, and when they were between the two lines of Anishnabeg fighters, Beedut's hand went down in the signal for attack.

But then – before he could utter his war cry – Beedut felt a fire in his back. The burning pain choked the war cry from his throat and drew away his strength. He pitched forward to the ground, while everything faded around him. The shrieks of his companions were as faint as echoes. The forest disappeared. The only reality was the terrible fire in his back – and he twisted and writhed, striving to be rid of it. Finally, like everything else, it faded; and Beedut sensed that his being was in flight. Light as a feather he travelled, going down, down, down – through a dark and infinite void.

Gradually, the blackness began to lift; and soon Beedut passed from darkness into light. He had entered a new and different reality. He was beside the Path of Souls.

In front of him was a column of spirits, countless men and women passing from the left to the right. On either side more human spirits appeared, hurrying to join the throng. Beedut looked on the procession in wonder; and then, urged by some force, he advanced to join the column. But the men and women turned on him in loathing. "Vanquished!" they hissed. "Abandoned!" Beedut did not belong with them.

Fleeing, Beedut passed into yet another level of reality. On this level, he could see and he could hear and he could smell – but he could not feel. He saw the trees and the clouds and the earth. He heard the rush of wind and the song of birds. He smelled the fresh scent of the forest. He sensed everything just as he had in life – except now he was unable to touch or to feel any of it. This was the third level.

On the ground below him, Beedut saw a body. It was

twisted and torn, its face pressed against the earth. Three arrows were buried in its back, and blood welled from the wounds. The entire body was engulfed in blue flame, a flame that pulsed, ebbing and flowing. Yet the strange fire neither charred the body nor scorched the dry leaves of the forest floor. Beedut marvelled at the sight. The body and the trees around it should have been black and burning.

A little further away lay another body, still clutching its war club. Its distorted face was red with blood from a terrible wound, and its chest and arms were pierced with arrows. This body, too, was enveloped with fire – but here the flames were of crimson and gold. As they licked about the corpse the bright flames ate away flesh, dissolving tissue and fibre and marrow. They strove to annihilate everything.

Beedut was about to look away from the destruction when the designs upon the figure's clothing caught his attention. They seemed familiar ... like the markings on the war club seemed familiar. With sudden horror, Beedut recognized his friend and companion. One of the men he had invited to come with him on the War Path was being dissolved by fire before his eyes.

Beedut stared again at the other body. Now, although he could not see its face, he recognized the clothing and the weapons. They were his! It was *his* body that lay sprawled on the ground. He, Beedut, was looking at himself. He was seeing his whole body for the very first time.

Transfixed by this spectacle, Beedut was overcome by awe and then by fear. Was it a vision? How could he be separated from his body when it should have been a part of him and he a part of it? And then, gradually, Beedut realized that it was not an illusion. It was his own flesh there below him, motionless and pierced by arrows. Some force had driven him from it; and some mystery allowed him to retain his senses. As he looked at his body from the outside Beedut knew that he had become something else – another being, another substance. Only if he could be united again with his body would he be a man once more.

Fiercely, scorning the ice-blue glow of the flames, Beedut hurled himself into his body. But still he could feel nothing. And for the second time he was overwhelmed by absolute darkness, stripped of consciousness, pulled, fragile as a feather, into a black void. When light returned he was again standing outside his body, rejected by his own flesh and his own form.

Filled with pity for the body he had left, Beedut recalled the circumstances that had caused it to lie there among the leaves. Instead of Beedut and his war party ambushing the Dakota – it was they who had been ambushed. Instead of being the victors they were the vanquished. For Beedut, it was a loss of reputation, for he had disregarded the advice of the medicine man and placed glory above the safety of his men. But worse than the defeat or the dishonour was the abandonment. He and his companion had been ignored by the war party, left behind to be reviled by their enemies or eaten by the crows and the worms. A careless war chief – Beedut now lay forgotten and disgraced.

Outraged, Beedut turned away from his body and set off through the forest in search of his surviving companions. He would have revenge on the war party for the way it had treated him. As he travelled, Beedut noticed that he could see the soul/spirits of the animals and the birds. Even the trees seemed somehow transparent. But the angry warrior paused for nothing in his search. He passed the homeward bound and triumphant Dakota warriors – but they were of less interest to him than his own men. He passed three more of his companions lying broken and bleeding on the ground – but even this sight could not lessen his bitterness. Beedut was resolved on revenge.

At last he came upon the four survivors. Huddled among the trees they were moaning from the pain of their wounds and trying to bind the injuries with buckskin. Beedut strode directly to his cousin, a man who had a reputation as a fierce warrior. "Why did you run away?" he shouted. "Why didn't you wait? Why did you leave me to be fought over by crows and reviled by the spirits?" The stinging questions came in torrents, but Beedut's cousin seemed unable to hear. He kept tending to his wounds, as if he were deliberately ignoring Beedut.

"Why didn't you help?" Beedut cried again. "Why don't you go back for me?" And when his cousin only closed his eyes in weariness, Beedut struck him across the face as hard as he could.

Instead of reeling from the blow, Beedut's cousin only shivered. "Did you feel that sudden cold?" he murmured to the warrior beside him. "Or is it just my wounds ...."

Recoiling, Beedut suddenly realized that although he could see and hear his companions, they did not know he was there. There was a barrier between the level he was on and the level of living beings that no form of communication could cross. And yet, unless he could reveal his circumstances to his people, his still-living body would be left to the weather and the animals. After death, his bones would be scattered. Unable to ever redeem his defeat, his name would be tarnished, and he would be remembered only in insinuating whispers.

Despairing, Beedut returned to his prostrate body. And now, in the branches of the trees around it, he saw the black shadows of waiting crows. Again, he strove to re-enter and re-animate his flesh – and this time he almost succeeded. He gained the ability to feel. He felt the arrows in his back and a parched burning in his throat. But then the pain itself overwhelmed him, casting him into darkness.

When, for the third time, Beedut's spirit awoke on the third level, he felt a strange sensation. It was as if he were being drawn and summoned. A force pulled him away from the place where his body lay. Without knowing what the force was, Beedut yielded to it willingly.

He found himself transported to a village that he recognized. He was led to a lodge that he knew had been his home. Gathered within was his family, the men with their faces blackened in mourning, the women keening in sorrow. Beedut wanted to clasp them all. He wanted to talk to them. But most of all, he wanted to go to his wife's side. Nearing his wife, he whispered to her – but she did not hear. He reached out to touch her – but his touch made her shudder as if at a sudden chill. She clutched at her mother for comfort.

"Hush," said her mother. "Hush. He is dead. And no one can help him."

"But I want him back," cried Beedut's wife. "He is mine. He belongs here. If you leave him there then I will go to him myself!"

"Hush," said her mother. "You cannot go. But ... since you want the body of your husband so much ... your father and your uncle will go."

It was the love and the remembrance of his wife that would save Beedut from his journeyings between the Land of the Living and the Land of Souls. With his hope and strength renewed, Beedut returned to his body, and for the third time he attempted to enter it. This time he was not rejected by his flesh; and as he lingered in the darkness he dreamed. He met a spirit who told him that he had not been buried as befitting a warrior, and that was why he had been forced to wander. A warrior, said the spirit, must be buried in a sitting position facing west. He must wear his battle dress; and he must have his weapons at his side – as if he could be ready in an instant to do battle. The Anishnabeg must never forget to bury their dead, warned the spirit. And for four days, a fire must be kept burning on the grave mound. The flame would keep the soul/spirit warm as it changed from one state to another, and moved from one dimension to the next.

The search party sent by Beedut's wife found Beedut where he had fallen. The medicine man who had once warned Beedut against the War Path, now removed the arrows from his back and applied poultices to the wounds. In a few days, Beedut regained consciousness. When he had recovered fully, he told the people of his wanderings and of his meeting with the spirit. And the people promised to always abide by the ritual and perform the rites of burial.

PREPARATION FOR THE SECOND INSTRUCTION

The circle of mourners around Zhawaeshk's body continued their watch as the sun set and the light dimmed. Eventually, the men returned from their task of digging the grave, and a fire was lit against the darkness. Soon afterwards, Mishi-Waub-Kaikaik also returned, and sat again in his place beside the body. He chanted:

K'neekaunissinaun, zunugut ae-nummook.
Our brother, difficult is the road.

K'neekaunissinaun, mino-waunigoziwinning

141

k'd'weekimmigoh.
Our brother, you are invited to the Happy Land.

"Our brother!" said Mishi-Waub-Kaikaik. "Before you set out, let me tell you about the Path of Souls. Listen – for it is dangerous! But you have nothing to fear if you do not yield to the temptations.

"You will see a trail before you. It is this trail that we know as the Path of Souls. It leads from the east to the west; and we see it in the sky at night. Kineu (War Eagle) of our tribe walked on that path and returned to tell us of his journey. Listen, and hear how close his account is to the tales told by our elders...."

THE STORY OF KINEU

It was a long journey to the Path of Souls. When Kineu arrived, he saw in front of him a column of shadows and shapes. They were spirits; grey as dusk, yet dressed in their finest garments as if they were going to a festival. And the spirits performed slow dances, each in a different rhythm.

Kineu went to join them, because he thought that he was bound for the same destination. But as soon as he took his first step towards the procession, the shadows hissed at him. They drew back, covering their eyes with their hands and waving him away. And so Kineu took another path, narrower than the one travelled by the spirits but leading in the same direction.

As soon as Kineu set out he saw a figure far ahead of him. At once he began to run in long, loping strides, hoping to overtake the stranger and have companionship along the way. As Kineu reduced the distance between himself and the figure, he saw that the stranger was tiny in stature, and that he was bent beneath the weight of a heavy burden. Curious, Kineu redoubled his pace; but before he could come any closer, the little stranger turned. When he saw Kineu he, too, began to run; and no matter how much Kineu strained he could not overtake the tiny figure. Whenever Kineu increased his pace, the stranger did as well. He was Kineu's equal in speed and endurance; and the distance between them would have remained unchanged had the stranger not at last stopped running and begun again to walk.

When Kineu finally approached the small figure, he discovered that it was a child of about two years old. The child was bowed under the weight of the cradle-board to which he was lashed; and as he walked, he whimpered. Kineu looked into the child's face. Beyond the tearless eyes was a sadness not of the present. It was not intense; but it was enduring. Urged by sudden compassion, Kineu determined to release the child and to comfort him; but when Kineu reached out, the child darted away. Twice more Kineu attempted to touch the child. And twice more the child retreated beyond his grasp. As the child wished, Kineu left him to bear his burden alone.

Without company, Kineu continued on his way. On either side of his trail was a forest, lush and beautiful; while ahead a luminous globe hung just above the tops of the trees, emitting a dazzling blue glow. This was the light that all must follow – the light that led to the Land of Souls. It was the light that those on earth saw at night in the northern skies. But soon there was something else that entranced Kineu: the thunder of a nearby river. It was unseen; yet the roar of its waters was both awesome and comforting. Kineu surrendered himself completely to the sound. He lingered. He stopped. He let the compelling, soothing voice of the water wash over him ....
And then, remembering the luminous globe, he renewed his journey. And the sound of the river, always to his left, accompanied him.

Not long after leaving the little child, Kineu came upon a camp. The people were eating. When they saw Kineu they invited him to sit down and to share their venison and whitefish, but he declined. None of their entreaties could divert him from his course. Some force urged him forward.

A little further along the trail there was a festival. Men and women were chanting and drumming, dancing and laughing. They summoned Kineu with glad cries and with the wave of their arms. But as much as he would have liked to tarry and celebrate, Kineu reluctantly moved on.

From a glade came a woman's voice, soft and alluring. "Come!" the sweet voice said. "Lie with me." Kineu stopped to look at the maiden. She was lithe and supple; copper skinned, tawny haired, and scented as if she had bathed in musk. She touched his arm gently. "Come!" she said again. "Rest with me awhile." Were it not for the beckoning light of the blue globe, Kineu would have yielded.

Further along, he found his way blocked by immense, writhing serpents. They reared before him and hissed fiercely; but Kineu was daunted only for a moment. He walked directly towards the serpents – and they retreated, drawing their coils from the path.

Kineu pressed on, witnessing natural and supernatural occurrences on every side. But no matter what the event or experience, there was always the rush of the river to his left and the radiant sphere ahead of him. Alternately walking and running, Kineu followed the trail. At last it slanted upward, climbed over a ridge, and curved leftward – down into the valley of the river.

On the river's bank, Kineu stopped to consider his course. The trail he had been following led to a log that was extended from bank to bank across the river – a bridge that pitched and rolled above the frothing, thundering water. Above the log bridge was stretched a vine hung with glowing, irridescent gourds that rattled upon the slightest of motions. And on the river's other bank, flanking each side of the bridge, lay two immense beasts. They were sleeping now; but at the sound of the gourds they would be ready to leap upon a stranger.

How was he to cross the bridge? How was he to silence the gourds? How was he to elude the beasts? Kineu did not know. Of one thing only was he certain: he was powerless to choose another course. His path, the path of all, had been determined long before.

And so, Kineu began to cross. Several times he lost his balance, and clung to the shaking bridge while the river raged and roared below. Each time, he regained his position, and began again to inch his way forward. He lay on his stomach – and not once during his tortuous passage did he disturb one of the gourds. Breathless, he finally reached the opposite bank; and with swift, silent feet, he slipped by the guardian beasts.

Once in the safety of the forest behind the animals, Kineu resumed his running. Now he travelled faster than before, moving uphill towards the crest of the valley's ridge, not stopping until he had gained the height. Here he paused to recover his breath and his strength, and to look at the scene below. Ahead of him stretched another valley and yet another ridge – but when Kineu saw what was in this valley, he knew that he no longer had far to travel. A village lay there: a village larger than any Kineu had heard of in stories; a village larger than any he had ever seen. Lodges, bright in the sunlight, covered the entire slope of the valley. And yet, in spite of all the dwellings and all the fireplaces, there was not a single man, woman, or child to be seen. The village was empty of all life.

At the very foot of the hill was a single lodge. It lay to one side of the path that led directly into the centre of the village, and it was a little larger than all the other lodges. Kineu looked at it for a long time. He would go there, he decided, before he entered the village.

But when he had descended the ridge, and when he finally stood at the entrance to the largest lodge, Kineu found that he was uncertain. He hesitated before he stepped forward to push aside the door flap. In the building's dim interior, he could make out one thing: the figure of an old woman.

The woman drew back from him, as the dancing spirits had done. "Why did you come here?" she hissed. "Don't you know where you are? You don't belong here! Go back!"

"Why?" Kineu asked. "What place is this?"

"This is the Land of Souls. This is the Land of Peace. This is the Village of Souls. You do not belong here. You are mortal. Go! Now!"

The old woman's whisper had almost risen into a shriek; but Kineu made no move to leave. He did not understand.

"You do not belong here," the old woman repeated harshly. "Only spirits live here. This is their home; and outsiders are not permitted. When you become a spirit like the rest you, too, will be allowed to stay. Then this will be your home. Until then, you must return to your proper home and exhaust your mortal existence." The old woman reflected a little. "It is strange," she went on, "that you did not tumble into the River of Souls as many have done; or that the monsters did not tear you apart, as they have torn others who tried to slip by them …. Ah, but then you are young and innocent. You have not

145

had time to wrong your brothers or your sisters or to injure the animals. See? I have told you how you must live. On your return to your world you must be kind to everyone, and you will know peace. Then someday – but not too soon – you will join your ancestors."

Suddenly, another voice spoke at the entrance to the lodge. "The spirits will dance tonight," the voice announced. "Your grandson is invited."

For a moment the old woman and Kineu looked at each other, and then the old woman shook her head. She addressed Kineu with the term that had been used by the mysterious voice. "My grandson!" she said. "You cannot leave after all. First, you must go to the festival – you cannot refuse the invitation. I wish you had heeded my warning. By the time the festival is over it may be too late ...." She paused, thinking. "My grandson! You must do exactly as I say. Do not dance. And do not eat or drink anything that the celebrants may offer you. You are only to watch. If you do not heed these instructions I cannot say what may happen to you. Do you understand?"

When Kineu promised that he would follow her advice, the old woman proceeded to tell him about existence in the Land of Souls. Never were its inhabitants hungry or thirsty or sad. Always, they feasted and rested. Each night, the spirits celebrated a festival by feasting, chanting, and dancing until dawn. Then, tired and spent, they withdrew to their lodges to sleep and to rest; preparing to rise again at dusk and start afresh. There was always some event or occasion to commemorate as fully and wholly as if it were the first.

When the old woman had finished her account she ate – but she did not offer Kineu any of her food. Even before she had finished her meal, the soft music of distant flutes echoed across the village. "Soon," said the old woman, "your cousins will come for you. They will take you to the festival. Be careful."

Kineu nodded. And soon, as the old woman had said, there was the sound of laughter and the calling of many voices outside the lodge. "Come!" they cried. "We are waiting!" Kineu stepped out. Around the lodge were his ancestors. Some of them he recognized; but others were unknown to him. As soon

146

as he appeared, the laughter subsided. "The air reeks of human flesh!" cried one of his cousins. "He must be cleansed!"

The men, Kineu's uncles, took him aside to a purification lodge. When he emerged a short time later, he put on new clothing made especially for him by his aunts. Dressed in the finest clothing that he had ever worn, Kineu was ready.

As the procession set out for the Central Festival Lodge, a young man began to walk beside Kineu. Big and strong, this young man would be Kineu's escort during the festival. All around Kineu the women laughed and sang, their glistening hair worn ankle-length. The men, their head-dress plumes waving, blew on their flutes and tapped their drums. All were spirits in essence and substance, but physical beings in form.

At the Sacred Festival Grounds there was already a large assembly feasting on venison, moose, trout, whitefish, partridge, corn, and wild rice. Still others were dancing around the Central Festival Pole and the Central Fire, accompanied by the pipe of flutes and the rhythm of drums. And though it should have been night, it was almost as light as day. The flame of the fire was so bright that it lit the northern skies.

Immediately, Kineu's companions joined in the feast, leaving him to stand to one side to watch. The young man who was his escort stood silently next to him. As soon as a spirit offered food, or extended a hand in an invitation to dance, the escort would step forward protectively. Without the intervention of his companion, Kineu would most certainly have joined in the feasting and the dancing.

As the night wore on, the laughter and the drumming, the piping and the dancing, increased in pitch and intensity. Kineu noticed that all those who danced were disfigured. Some were headless, some armless, a few were one-legged, and several were blind. Many bore gashes across their faces, scars upon their chests, or slashes upon their backs. Yet neither wounds nor deformities impaired the joy or the vigour of the celebrants.

On and on the spirits danced without tiring. The drums throbbed and the flutes pierced the air. Only when the night began to fade before the arrival of dawn did the music falter and the dancing flag. When this happened, Kineu's escort touched him on the arm. "Come," he said kindly. "It is time to go. The festival is almost over." And he took Kineu as far as the large lodge before disappearing into the coming dawn.

The old woman was waiting for Kineu. "You saw the Dance of the Maimed," she explained to him. "The dance of those crippled or murdered or mutilated or killed in battle. They wanted to commemorate their conquest of suffering and death.

"In some ways, things here are much the way they are in the Land of the Living. As they loved to celebrate events through festivals on earth, so spirits love to commemorate earthly triumphs in the Land of Souls. Feasting and dancing and singing make spirits happy. That is why there is a festival every night. And this night past, the lamed and the maimed presented their festival. Tomorrow evening it will be the turn of the infants; and the next night, the hunters. Each festival is conducted by different spirits. There are also festivals to celebrate new arrivals, when entire families gather together ...."

The old woman waited while Kineu changed out of his fine clothes, and while the quiet of morning gradually settled over the village. Then she stood, and lifted the flap from the lodge door. "Now that you know what it is like here, you must go," she said. "And if you follow the Path of Life as it is understood by the elders, you will return here one day. Come. I will show you the way back."

Outside the lodge, the woman pointed to the east over the crest of the ridge. "That is your way back," she told him. "Over the hill you will see the sphere of brightness. It will lead you. Follow it; and do not delay. Your parents will be glad to see you. And remember! Whenever you see the northern skies lit with light – think of the Land of Souls. Go now!"

On the other side of the ridge, the luminous globe reappeared on the horizon to the east. Following it, Kineu ran. Now there was no river and no bridge to cross; and yet it was the same trail that he had previously taken. He passed the child, still whimpering as it carried its cradle-board. He passed other travellers, who stepped aside when they saw him, and covered their eyes with their hands. Finally, he reached a spot where the globe stopped, shining even more brightly as it stood, motionless, above the path.

As Kineu watched, the globe changed shape, dissolving from a sphere into a column of fire. On either side, the lush green forests disappeared. All that was left was the trail beneath Kineu's feet – and it led directly into the pillar of flames. Kineu hesitated for just a moment. And then he hurled himself into the middle of the fire.

He had passed back into his own body.

THE PATH OF SOULS

After he had narrated the story of Kineu, Mishi-Waub-Kaikaik paused briefly. Then he again addressed the spirit of Zhawaeshk.

"Our brother! Soon you will be there in the Land of Souls. You will see your ancestors and your brothers and sisters. Already they are preparing a reception for your arrival. The men are hunting and fishing; the women are setting up your lodge and making clothes for you. When you arrive everything will be ready; and the spirits will celebrate the Festival of a New Arrival. And then you, too, will await the arrival of your wife and children.

"But before you arrive in the Land of Souls you must walk the Path of Souls. You must be careful. The trials that you endured on this Path of Life are over – but you will encounter new ones on every hill and at every bend along the Path of Souls. You are being tested. Be strong. Do not weaken.

"Listen, our brother! The tests that you will meet on the way are different from the ones that you suffered on earth. Here, they were direct and easily recognized. Although they were sometimes sudden, they were easily repelled. But the tests that you will face on the Path of Souls are not so plain. They are subtle, disguised in innocence. They are much more dangerous than any that you may have encountered in this life.

"Remember. Walk alone; eat by yourself; sleep with no one. Do this, even though there are hardships. You will be hungry and you will be cold. You will be lonely and you will be tired. You will be thirsty and you will be afraid. Your spirit will be weak. And when it is weak, the tests will appear.

"They will seem harmless. There may be a feast in a village

to which you will be invited. Do not go: it is the Feast of Death. There may be a night camp in which people are preparing for sleep. Do not stop: it is the Sleep of Death. If you come upon a campfire, do not warm yourself: it is the Fire of Death. If you see a brook, do not drink of it: it is the Water of Death. Should you come upon someone lying on the ground, leave him: it is the Agony of Death. Whatever you see or hear—pass it by.

"Our brother! Be on guard! Have a safe journey!"

Mishi-Waub-Kaikaik had finished his instructions. There was a moment of silence, and then he got to his feet. Before leaving the gathering, he went to each of the mourners and offered them his hand. After he had gone, the others remained with the body. They would stay there until dawn. And the older people would talk to Zhawaeshk as Mishi-Waub-Kaikaik had done.

THE INTERNMENT

In the morning, when droplets of dew were still hanging from the leaves of the trees, the burial procession set out for the grave that had been dug the day before. Four men carried the bark-encased body of Zhawaeshk, accompanied by Mishi-Waub-Kaikaik, the two attending women, and the gathering of mourners.

When the site was reached, the two women spread a rush mat in the bottom of the grave. With the help of the bearers, they placed Zhawaeshk's body upon the mat and arranged it in a sitting position, facing west. On his right side, the men placed his weapons and hunting equipment. On the left, they arranged his pipe, tobacco, and flints; a cooking vessel, a bowl, and a spoon; a blanket and some corn. Attached to his belt was his medicine bundle.

Mishi-Waub-Kaikaik began to chant:

K'neekaunissinaun, ani-maudjauh.
Our brother, he is leaving.

K'neekaunissinaun, cheeby-meekunnaung.
Our brother, on the Path of Souls.

As Mishi-Waub-Kaikaik chanted, the men began to fill the

150

grave, flinging in a handful of earth at a time. The earth sprayed against the birch bark like sleet, echoing in finality. One by one the women got up to dance the Dance of Burial and the Dance of Lament. Mishi-Waub-Kaikaik continued to chant:

K'neekaunissinaun, kego binuh-kummeekaen.
Our brother, do not stumble.

K'neekaunissinaun, k'gah odaessiniko.
Our brother, you will be welcome.

At last, the men had finished their work. Over the grave mound they erected a post engraved with the image of the bear, the totem of Zhawaeshk. The engraving was upside down, according to custom. While the women went for food, the men constructed a small lodge of birch bark, anchoring it with stones. It represented a temple in which the soul/spirit of Zhawaeshk could find shelter and refuge. When the structure was complete, the women returned with portions of meat, corn, wild rice, and water, and placed these offerings in front of the entrance to the shelter. Finally, the women built a small fire, and the mourners sat in a circle around the grave.

It was time to begin a vigil for the dead.

THE WATCH

For a time there was quiet around the grave. And then the older men and women began to take turns addressing Zhawaeshk. An old man spoke first.

"You were a warrior," he said. "Many times you performed the War Dance and took the war club on our behalf. Our lives were dear to you – as yours was to us – but it was your duty, your calling, to give your life for the tribe. When you fell, you fell as warriors wish, in battle .... The scars that you bore and the wounds that you felt shall ever remind us of your courage and your sacrifice – just as the plumes in your head-dress were the emblems of your worth and triumphs. On such as you do the weak depend. On such as you do the strong trust. On such as you can the people rest their lives.

"We grieve that you cannot remain with us. But it is the will of Kitche Manitou. Each man, each woman, is allotted a span of life and a quantity of good to fulfil. And although we may regard your span of life as all too brief, the good that you performed was more than that expected of any man or woman.

"No longer will we see your wounds, hear your war cry, look upon your head-dress, or take comfort in your presence. Only your memory remains. We shall honour you tomorrow, and all tomorrows, as long as we shall live."

After the words, there was silence. And then an old woman spoke.

"You were a good hunter. Never did you go out hunting without bringing back some game. Your wife and your children never went hungry. The elders and the poor looked to you. And as you were kind to the poor – so was Kitche Manitou good to you. As you honoured the spirit of the deer and the beaver, the whitefish and the trout, the duck and the partridge – so were they unselfish with you. You were good to us: and we thank you."

"You were a good son," another woman said. "Since you were a child you listened to your grandparents, to your father and mother and to the elders, always doing what was good. And as you were a good son, you were also a good companion to your wife and a good father to your children. You were kind. May our children be as dutiful as you were. We thank you and we will remember."

A second man raised his voice. "Needjee! (My friend!) We met a long time ago. Our soul/spirits met and touched and formed a bond. From the first they moved towards one another. We grew up together, you and I. We did things together. When we ran and wrestled – I was glad when you were the best. When I killed my first partridge and my first deer – you asked me to show you how. We became men and were friends still: you, a warrior; I, a hunter. I accompanied you on the War Path when you asked me. You came with me into the hills to hunt deer and bear, and to the rivers to spear fish. My soul/spirit goes with you; yours stays with me. My friend! I miss you ...."

For four days and four nights the gathering of men and women tended the grave fire and kept watch by the grave. At the end of that time, the soul/spirit of Zhawaeshk had fully completed its transformation into spirit. And only then did the vigil come to an end.

THE PERIOD OF MOURNING

After the vigil, the two attending women led Zhauwoonoquae, the widow, back to her lodge. Because Zhawaeshk's spirit would be with her, Zhauwoonoquae was not to look upon a man, or be in the company of a man, for a year. The women reminded Zhauwoonoquae of this, and she nodded silently in answer. She knew the code. A man who had lost his wife would keep the same one year period of mourning.

Within the lodge, the women unbraided Zhauwoonoquae's hair, so that it would hang unadorned and free. They helped her remove her dress; and as they wrapped it in a birch bark packet, Zhauwoonoquae replaced it with old, worn clothing. Next, the women looped a braided buckskin around Zhauwoonoquae's neck, and wound a thong over her left shoulder and under her right arm. On the thong was fastened the bark packet containing her dress. Not for one year was Zhauwoonoquae to change her garments or rebraid her hair or remove her symbols of mourning. Every evening she was to visit the grave of her departed companion-in-life in order to wail her grief; and, if she wished, she could lacerate herself.

Again, the women reminded Zhauwoonoquae of these things; and again the widow nodded silently in answer. Then, after the preparations were finished, the women left Zhauwoonoquae and went to her eldest son. Around the boy's eyes they painted black circles. Because he still lived at home with his mother, this sign of mourning also had to be worn for one year.

And so Zhauwoonoquae observed her period of mourning – not simply in observance of custom, but in real, heart-felt grief. During the year, all the articles that she made or that were presented to her as gifts became part of the spirit-bundle that she carried. Wrapped in birch bark, they were added to the first birch bark packet that contained the dress she had worn on the day of Zhawaeshk's burial. Eventually, the bundle contained a pair of moccasins, a blanket, a jacket, leggings, gauntlets, a pipe, tobacco, games, and feathers.

When a year had passed, Zhauwoonoquae took her children and went to the lodge of Zhawaeshk's parents. Following custom, she asked them to release her from the outward signs of mourning, even though her sorrow for her husband would remain. Zhawaeshk's parents agreed; and his mother came forward, lifted the heavy spirit-bundle, and untied the cord that bound it to Zhauwoonoquae's side. "You are a worthy daughter," she said. "You were a good companion for Zhawaeshk. Go now, and start afresh! In four days we shall celebrate the Restoration of the Mourner Festival."

Now, Zhauwoonoquae could open her spirit-bundle. And when she appeared on the fourth day she was dressed in new garments and her hair was smoothly braided. It was Mishi-Waub-Kaikaik, as the medicine man who had presided over her husband's burial rites, who spoke to welcome Zhauwoonoquae and her family back into the life of the village.

"For a year," he said, "this woman and her children have been in mourning. For a year they have not celebrated a single festival – for those in mourning must abstain unless invited. And today we do invite them. We invite them to eat with us, to dance with us, and to laugh with us. We share with them our joy...."

But even though Zhauwoonoquae had been released from her period of mourning, she still continued to visit Zhawaeshk's grave. And even though she married again and loved again, she would always honour her first husband.

The Council

Zuguswediwin

THE WARNING

Yes. The village had heard. Though the reports were rumours only – and almost too astonishing to be true – they were still disturbing. There were so many refugees from the east who told of displacement and dispossession that there had to be some substance to the stories. Something was happening. Something was compelling people to leave their homes. Occasionally, villagers would question the accounts; and then the refugees would shake their heads and declare, with the certainty of prophets: *Your turn will come! You will lose your homes! You, too, will be wanderers!*

But those who listened only laughed. It was too impossible to believe.

THE FIRST PROPOSAL

And then, a few years later, an officer came to the village. He was escorted by an entourage of aides and soldiers and accompanied by an interpreter. Through the interpreter, the officer told Chief Ningiziwaush (Great Blue Heron) and his people that the Great White Father had empowered him to make a treaty with the Indians for the lands in the immediate area, and for an additional tract, extending north and west, whose extent could only be reckoned by the number of days of travel. In return for the surrender of these lands, the Great White Father would present the Indians with gifts: clothing, firearms, powder, cloth, medicines, rope, blankets, kettles,

157

pipes, tobacco, knives, rum, combs, fish hooks, nets, hoes, mirrors, scissors, thread, and needles. Moreover, the Great White Father would give the tribe money. A certain sum would be paid immediately upon their consent to the treaty; and thereafter, a fixed sum would be paid, in perpetuity, to each member of the tribe.

The offer appeared to be generous, even though Ningiziwaush and his advisers could not understand the maps on which the lands were outlined. Certain members of the tribe wanted very much to agree but, finally, Ningiziwaush declined. He did not have the authority, he said, to sell the land or to make any agreement binding upon his fellow chiefs. He promised the officer that he would convene a general council asking the chiefs of the tribes residing in the area coveted by the Great White Father to consider the proposal. Later, in the autumn, the officer himself could summon the chiefs in order to hear their final answer. The officer agreed. After he left, Ningiziwaush sent his courier to deliver an urgent message to Mishi-Pizheu (Great Lynx), chief of the nearest village.

THE SUMMONING TO COUNCIL

It was not easy delivering messages. There were no trails in that endless tract of forest. Pine shaded into maple; maple gave way to cedar; cedar blended with spruce; spruce merged into birch ... and all were governed only by the slow, inevitable laws of growth. The land on which the trees rooted was uneven and rugged. There were sloping hills, and crags of rock that fell sharply into narrow gorges. There were worn, winding ridges, and steep escarpments. There were green-blue lakes and brown swamps and yellow marshes; and there were crystal clear rivers that curved across meadows, swept through valleys, or spilled over rocky cliffs. Incomparably beautiful, yet difficult to cross, was the land.

The people themselves did not make it easy to pass messages from tribe to tribe. In the summer they ranged far and wide, often beyond summons; and even were they to receive notice of a meeting they would hesitate, in a natural distrust of haste and urgency. The pace of their life, like the life of the natural growth around them, was slow and unhurried.

But this time, the courier was lucky. He was able to deliver his message to Mishi-Pizheu, and to convince him that the matter was urgent. He gave the chief a small bundle of sticks, one of which was to be thrown away each day in order to keep track of time and remember the date of the council. For his part, Mishi-Pizheu sent his personal courier to the chief of the next village – who would, in turn, dispatch his own messenger. In this way, everyone would eventually be notified.

Meanwhile, Ningiziwaush's village prepared for the arrival of the delegations by killing extra game and fish. As hosts, the people were obliged to provide as well as they were able for their guests, friends and strangers alike – not only out of custom but out of simple goodwill. In fact, councils such as this were often occasions for visiting relatives and friends.

Days before the date of the council, the chiefs and their attendants began to arrive. They came early to talk, to visit, and to feast before they began to discuss the important matters in formal council. There was Mishi-Pizheu of the Eagle Totem, chief of the Heavy Elm People; Mishi-Waub-Kaikaik of the Bear Totem, medicine man and chief of the Cataract People; Mazinininh (Carved Image of Man) of the Caribou Totem, warrior and chief of the Fire River People; Mizaun (Thistle) of the Pike Totem, chief of the Black Forest Dwellers; and Neezhawayaush (Flies Twice) of the Sucker Totem, chief of the North Portage Dwellers. Ningiziwaush of the Hawk Totem – chief of the Sand Dunes Dwellers and of the village where the council was gathered – was the most senior of the chiefs. It was because he was the leading spokesman of the area that the White Man's delegation had come first to him. Still, in the days before the council, the first subject of discussion among the chiefs and their peoples was not the proposal of the officer but the abundance of the season's game and berries. The coming winter would be easy.

THE INVOCATION

On the morning of the council, a member of the Keepers of the Fire kindled the fire that would burn during the meetings. The

159

chiefs, with their councillors and couriers, sat in a circle around the flames. Behind this circle was the audience, waiting to listen to the orators.

The Keeper of the Pipe unfolded the leather casing that bound the sacred pipe. He filled the bowl with a tobacco mixture used only in special ceremonies, and lit the pipe for Ningiziwaush. The significance of this ritual came from the smoking of the pipe performed by the spirit Nanabush and his father Epingishmook – an act which symbolized the end of conflict and the beginning of peace between them. Thereafter, the ritual of the smoking of the pipe was an essential part of every conference, performed before deliberations began in order to induce temperance in speech and wisdom in decision. It was for this reason that councils, both general and local, were called Zuguswediwin (The Smoking of the Pipe).

As the people watched, Ningiziwaush took the pipe from the keeper and began to speak.

"Our Great Mystery! You have bestowed upon us much. You have created the land on which we live – the land which is our Mother and to which we belong. You have created the deer and the beaver and the whitefish and the grouse – creatures who have given their lives so that we may eat this day. You have extended our own lives, so that all of us who have met before could meet here yet again; and you have given us a good day for our meeting .... We have been asked to consider parting with some of the gifts that you have given us. But we do not know whether we have the right to part with what is not ours – as we would part with a coat or a pipe or a bow. Hence we meet today. We come to you for guidance.

"Mother Earth! We honour you. Whatever we have we get from you. The deer that we eat are from your forests, and the waters that we drink are from your valleys. We see beauty in your hills and hear songs in your winds and feel a caress in the ground you place under our feet. You possess everything; we possess nothing. You give us all; and we can only give you honour in return. Accept, in this fragrant smoke, our gratitude."

Ningiziwaush paused and blew a whiff of smoke from the pipe. Then he blew four more puffs, one for each of the four corners of the world.

"To you who reside and dwell to the north: give us foresight in our deliberations this day! As the animals build their shelters before the coming of winter, and as the birds seek refuge before the approach of storm, let us also know the future so that we can prepare. Our minds are clouded; and we gather today so that what is too big for one mind may be understood by many. We need to see beyond the mountain, to discover the direction of the trail, and to know whether the weather will be fair .... Open our eyes and our ears and our minds so that we may do what is right for our people and for our children. Give us guidance.

"To you who reside and dwell to the west: give us the knowledge to understand the matters that we are to consider this day! We have come to put our minds and hearts together so we may know what ought to be done and what ought not to be done. We seek your guidance and strength so that we may speak as with one tongue, one voice.

"To you who reside and dwell to the south: help us use good judgement! What we must consider today is new and unknown. There is nothing in our past experience to guide us; there is nothing in our history to prepare us for the results of our decision. We are told that we will benefit, and we would like to believe this. But how may we know? How may we judge? There are many paths in life to follow, many choices to make. Many of them are true; and just as many are false. We must choose the right one, so that we do not bring hardship to our people and make conditions worse for our children. We appeal to you to counsel us in making the right decision, so that we may benefit our people.

"To you who reside and dwell to the east: give us the will and the strength to fulfil our decision no matter how difficult it may be! We are fearful and uneasy – and yet we must be true. Once a promise has been made there can be no turning back. If we agree to sell our lands, let us have the courage to abide by our agreement. If we refuse, let us have the courage to stand by our refusal. In this we need your guidance."

When Ningiziwaush had finished the invocation, he passed the pipe to the chief at his right. No words were said as the pipe was passed around until it returned to Ningiziwaush, who handed it back to the keeper. Then Ningiziwaush spoke again, using the formal phrase which began all Anishnabeg speeches.

"Neekaunissidoog! N'dawaemaudoog! (My brothers! My sisters!)" he said. "Let us listen to Mino-waewae recount our history."

Mino-waewae (The Good Voice), a tall, swarthy man, rose to his feet. He was the tribal storyteller, the historian who was asked to relate the history of the Anishnabeg on all formal occasions. An orator, he took hold of his listeners, first with his eyes and then with his presence. For Mino-waewae it was an easy thing to do; he had command of the language, command of the history, and above all, he had command of himself. He lived by, and thus reflected, the first principle of credibility and trust: *Talk not too much.* When Mino-waewae stood to recount the history of the Anishnabeg he was dealing with "truth" – the core of history and the proper subject matter of speech.

In all his years, Mino-waewae had never abused either the truth or his listeners. He spoke what he knew, and that was enough. He did not presume to go beyond his knowledge or to stretch or bend or warp it. In its whole and unaltered state it kept him, himself, true. He spoke only when the occasion warranted it, since to have spoken more often would have worn out and even blunted the truth. Instead, by infrequent speeches, he kept the truth of his accounts fresh, vital, and compelling. Mino-waewae spoke just long enough to inspire the yearning for more truth and to nourish the regard that was due to the truth. In all his speeches, Mino-waewae upheld the essential facts; he did not once belabour them, or bury them with the sounds of words. Of those who heard him speak, not one was ever heard to say: "He talks too much," or "He talks in circles," or "He is lost in his own mind." Instead, everyone could agree that: "He talks directly," and "He speaks the truth," and "He is eloquent."

Now, in the moments before Mino-waewae began speaking, he was taking hold of his audience. He was entering their spirits and drawing them to him gently, so that for the next half hour or so they would willingly follow him wherever he went, no matter how quickly or how slowly he led them.

THE HISTORY OF THE ANISHNABEG

Neekaunissidoog! N'dawaemaudoog! Before you begin your council, bear in mind the history of the people, so that you may find inspiration and strength in knowing who and what we are. It is the story of our forefathers and their deeds. We are the beneficiaries of their labours, and we must pass the memory of them on to our children. As our forefathers kept the memory of the past alive, so must we.

Before the beginning there was only the Great Mystery. Nothing else. And the Great Mystery beheld a vision. He saw the sun, the stars, and the earth; the mountains and valleys, rivers and lakes. He saw pines and grasses, corn and roses. He saw eagles and caribou, whitefish and fireflies, bears and men. He heard thunders and winds, laughter and weeping, torrents and drums and chants. He touched rock and water, fire and ice. He felt joy and sadness, contentment and disappointment. He tasted honey and iris, wild rice and sap. He sensed birth and growth, age and death .... Then the vision passed.

The Great Mystery had seen what had been unknown, unseen, nothing. The vision had to be fulfilled; not because it was in itself compelling, but because it was conceived in the mind of the Great Mystery. And so he brought rock and fire and wind and water into being. From these substances he created the sun and the stars and the earth and the seas.

Next he made the plants: forests and grasses, flowers and corn, wild rice and melons. After the plant-beings, he set animals upon the earth: the moose, the deer, the bear, and the dog. In the air he put the eagle, the crane, the goose, and the robin. Among the grasses he placed the grasshopper, the beetle, the snake, and the frog; while in the waters were located the whitefish, the trout, the sturgeon, the sucker, and the turtle.

Last, the Great Mystery created man.

To all the creatures had been given some of the mystery. The owl had sight; the sparrow hawk, swiftness; the flicker, music; the loon, a knowledge of the seasons; the deer, grace; the beaver, gentility; the sturgeon, swimming; the butterfly, beauty; the plants, growth and healing. But to man, the Great Mystery gave the capacity for vision.

Each creature had its portion of the mystery. Each creature had its place on earth, its time, and its purpose. This was the source of order and harmony. And then – something happened! The seas overran and engulfed the land. Only the water-animals and the fish and some birds survived. Man was destroyed.

Now, there was a woman spirit called Geezhigoquae (Sky Woman) residing alone in the skies. In her loneliness she asked the Great Mystery for a companion. The request was granted. Geezhigoquae and her companion lived together until she conceived.

Below, among the waters, the animals and the birds and the fish sensed that something extraordinary was happening to Geezhigoquae. They invited her to come down from the skies to rest upon the back of the great turtle, whom they had persuaded to rise to the surface. When Geezhigoquae had descended, she asked for a morsel of soil – and the muskrat, the least of the animals, at last brought up a pawful of soil from the depths. Geezhigoquae took the lump of earth and, with her finger, traced it around the rim of the turtle's shell. Then, she breathed upon it; and the soil spread, covering the turtle's back, growing into an island which our forefathers called Mishee Mackinakong (Place of the Great Turtle).

There, on the island, Geezhigoquae gave birth to twins, a boy and a girl. They were called Anishnabeg (Good Beings or Spontaneous Beings). Because Geezhigoquae was of the sky while her children were of the earth, it was at first difficult for her to take care of them. The bear, the grouse, the fisher, and the crow helped her to feed, clothe, shelter, and comfort the two babies; and finally, when they had grown up, Geezhigoquae returned to her home in the sky. Now, whenever the moon shines, we remember the first of mothers.

After Geezhigoquae returned to her home, the Anishnabeg lived on Mishee Mackinakong, growing in numbers. These were bright, happy days, filled with hope and laughter, good meals and quiet nights. Then, suddenly, the Anishnabeg began to get sick and to die off like mosquitoes in the autumn. There was no explanation and no cure for the epidemic – until the Great Mystery sent four spirits to the people to teach them wisdom and medicine.

Sired by Epingishmook (The West), and born of Winonah (To Nourish from the Breast), a mortal woman, each of the four spirits performed some deed and left a legacy for the benefit of the people. Mudjeekawiss (Starting Son), the eldest son, was the warrior. Big, strong, and mean-tempered, he spent his days patrolling the boundaries of the Land of the Anishnabeg. In defence of our people he vanquished the powerful Bear Tribe, wresting from them the wampum on which our forefathers inscribed their deeds. Papeekawiss (Son Who Breaks), the second son, was the artist. Handsome, lithe, and graceful, he was fond of ritual, dance, and adornment. He spent his days inventing new dances, designing elegant costumes, and refining and performing ceremonies. Sometimes, purely out of mischief, Papeekawiss would play pranks on his brothers. He brought a sense of beauty to our forefathers.

The third son was Chibiabos (Ghost Rabbit), who was quiet, gentle, and reflective. During the day he was by the water or out in the forests and meadows, where he listened to the cicadas or the sparrows or the wind and the waves. At night he came among the fires to sing and to chant to the beat of his drum. Chibiabos instilled into our people a love of harmony in music and song. The last son was Nanabush, an orphan. He was one of us and yet he also belonged to the spirit world. He would be man one time, and spirit another. He could be foolish, but he could also be wise and kind. During his life he taught us what we ought and ought not to do. He taught the art of healing and the manner of knowledge and the greatest of human virtues: kindness. His spirit is with us still.

When Nanabush was about a year old, his mother died. Old Nokomis (Grandmother) brought him up. Although she taught him everything she knew, she told him nothing about his ancestry. As Nanabush got older he heard rumours; and believing that his father had caused Winonah's death, he went on a journey, intending to search for his father and to kill him.

Father and son fought a bitter battle yet neither could overcome the other, no matter what stratagems or mystic powers they used. They were spirits ... gods ... and therefore equal. In the end, both grew weary of battle, and they agreed to a truce. Vowing nevermore to take up arms against each other they smoked, as a sign of their pledge, the Pipe of Peace. From that day to this our people have smoked the sacred pipe to allay passions and to invoke peace.

While our forefathers were still residing on Mishee Mackinakong, six Mystery Beings emerged from the lake and came to the shore of the island. They were suffering from starvation and exposure, and one of them collapsed and died on the beach. Our forefathers took pity on the five surviving strangers, and gave them food, clothing, and medicines until they recovered.

Although the Anishnabeg were abundantly kind, they were limited in their knowledge and in their experience of life. And so, as an expression of gratitude for the treatment they had received, the strangers taught our ancestors, showing that kindness begets kindness. Buzwaewae (Echo Making Bird) taught the principles and the art of leadership. Noka (Bear), warrior and guardian, imparted the forms and methods of defending the family and the tribe. Waubizhaezh (Marten) demonstrated the manner of providing for the family and for the community. Waussee (Sunfish) instilled the methods of teaching and learning. And Misheekaehn (Great Turtle) taught healing and communion with the spirit world. After the five Mystery Beings departed, our ancestors adopted their totems as symbols of the five basic functions of mankind. And the totems became bonds of brotherhood and unity among our people.

Gradually, our ancestors recovered from the ravages of the epidemic. They regained their vigour, and soon they were too numerous for their original home. Many left Mishee Mackinakong to occupy the land nearby or to journey beyond. East, west, north, and south they travelled, founding villages and towns on every side of Kitche-Ojibway-Gameeng (Great Sea of the Anishnabeg). In bays and narrows they settled, where whitefish teemed and deer ran in herds: Gaumeenautikawayauk (Place of Many Berries), Wausswaugunning (Place of Torch Fishing), Nipigong (Place of Waters), Boweting (Place of Rapids), Teemigameeng (Deep Lake), Nipissing (Place of the Elms), Kitche-Gaugeedjwung (Great Edge-Over), and Wauwi-Autinoong (Round Lake).

Expansion was peaceful. But there were other people, the Mundawaek (People of the Catbird), who resented the growth of our forefathers. In an attempt to repulse and to wipe out the Anishnabeg, the Mundawaek assembled a large force of men. Their warriors attacked our warriors; and our forefathers say that the battle raged for many days. Such was the violence of the fighting – and so desperate did the Mundawaek become – that they sent boys and girls into the battlefield. In the end our ancestors triumphed, adopting the Mundawaek survivors into the tribe. According to our ancestors, this war with the Mundawaek was the greatest and bloodiest conflict in which the Anishnabeg ever engaged. Never again was there such a war.

The story of our people does not end here. It goes on – it will continue to go on – and it is good, sometimes, to stop along the trail in order to rest and look back. We look back with pride and gratitude: pride in the courage and strength and deeds of our people; gratitude for the many things they have left us.

From the past and from our ancestors we have inherited a language harmonious to the ear, ceremonies edifying to attend, and traditions to be observed and continued. We are heirs to understandings and to insights into life and the nature of things. We have derived wisdom from the elders to guide us in the conduct of our affairs. Our legacy is indeed great. Let us never forget our debt to our ancestors. And let us always remember our duty to our children.

Mino-waewae sat down. For a long while the only sounds to be heard were the calls of birds and the crackle of the fire. Although Mino-waewae's words had faded away, the thoughts and the dreams that he had inspired lingered; and the men and women in his audience sat mute and transfixed. Not until the Keeper of the Fire moved to put more logs in the flames did they return to the present.

Ningiziwaush stood. "Neekaunissidoog! N'dawaemau-doog!" he said, looking at the faces around him. "We welcome you. You have come a long way in the acceptance of our invitation. You have left your villages and your homes – you have put by hunting and fishing and risked your food supplies – in order to attend this council. We are glad that you came.

"From your faces, and from the vigour of your steps, we can see that Kitche Manitou has been good to you. He has made your journey pleasant and easy. We thank Kitche Manitou for looking after you. And we ask him to safeguard you on your return home.

"Neekaunissidoog! N'dawaemaudoog! While you are with us, and for as long as you wish to stay, we shall share with you our fire, our food, our thoughts, and our laughter. You will not be cold or hungry or thirsty. We are glad to see you; and we hope that after the council you will remain with us to smoke the pipe of friendship and to renew the unity of spirit that binds us all.

"My fellow chief, Mishi-Waub-Kaikaik, was here when the White Men came to us. Now he will explain the purpose of the council."

Slowly, Mishi-Waub-Kaikaik stood up. He was old now, but he had been present when the officer had made the request for land to Ningiziwaush; and since that time he had given much thought to what such a proposal would mean to his people. When he spoke, his voice was deliberate and strong.

THE APPEAL

Neekaunissidoog! N'dawaemaudoog! A month or so ago, a delegation of White Men came to this village – just as some of our displaced brothers from the east had foretold.

They offered to buy the whole of our land for money and gifts; and they said that they would provide a sum of money each year thereafter for as long as the sun shines, the rivers flow, and the grasses grow. They said that land would be set aside for our homes and for our exclusive use; and that schools would be built and teachers provided for the instruction of our children and the betterment of our communities. They said that medicine, clothing, tools, and hunting equipment would be supplied to enhance our lives; and that farm implements would be given to us so that we, like them, could become farmers. They assured us that even if we surrendered our lands we could continue to hunt and to fish wherever and whenever it suited us. And they promised that the land set aside for our use would be kept safe and secure from trespass.

Since that meeting my dreams and my sleep have been disturbed, and my spirit has been troubled. I want to do what is right and just for both our people and the strangers ....

I remember the White Men saying that their people were poor, and that they needed the land for food, for the kindling of their fires, and for the well-being of their children. I do not wish to see elders and children hungry, ragged, or homeless. We should be kind.

But, I also remember our brothers from the east. They said that if we sold the land we would betray our own elders and our own children – as they had done. And I do not wish to beggar our own people. We all know that with all the land we now own and occupy, and with all the hunting territories that we possess, we still have disputes. How much sharper and more frequent will these disagreements become between ourselves – and between us and the White Men – as more people occupy the land!

Even if we were certain that our lives, like those of the White Men, would be enriched by the sale of our land – do we have the right to surrender it? If we give away the land we are giving away the rights of our children, because the land is a gift of the Great Mystery to our people. There is no gift to compare to the gift of the Great Mystery ... and to relinquish that gift to another would be like rejecting it. Our land was a gift to those who have gone and whose bones are interred within the earth, to those present whose feet stand yet upon the trails, and to those still to come. The ownership of our land rests with the whole tribe for as long as the tribal fire burns. When our generation passes, ownership comes to the next generation. That is the way it has always been. And that is the way it ought to be.

But the White Man thinks differently; and I do not understand him. Perhaps my mind is too small to hold these new ideas. To control and possess the land as the White Man wishes does not make sense. Can man possess a gust of the North Wind or a measure of flowing water? Can he control a mass of clouds or a herd of moose?

No. Do not mistake the truth. It is not man who owns the

land; it is land that owns man. And we, the Anishnabeg, were placed on this land. From beginning to end it nourishes us: it quenches our thirst, it shelters us, and we follow the order of its seasons. It gives us freedom to come and go according to its nature and its extent – great freedom when the extent is large, less freedom when it is small. And when we die we are buried within the land that outlives us all. We belong to the land by birth, by need, and by affection. And no man may presume to own the land. Only the tribe can do that.

Neekaunissidoog! N'dawaemaudoog! Do we have the right to sell our homeland? Do we have the right to rob our children of their claim to it? Do we have the right to sell the resting places of our ancestors? Do we have the right – even if we were agreed – to sell what is a gift of the Great Mystery, and what also belongs to those who will come after us? I cannot think so.

Neekaunissidoog! N'dawaemaudoog! What assurance do we have that our lives would be improved by the surrender of a portion of our homeland? We have none. Unless we judge correctly, our campfires and our tribal fire will be extinguished just as surely as the fires of our brothers and sisters to the east have been smothered.

Neekaunissidoog! N'dawaemaudoog! Some of our people are destitute – and we are told that some of the White Man's people are destitute also. We are told that by surrendering our homes, we will help both. I cannot understand how this can be. If we take from one to give to another, only the one who receives will be happy. The other is deprived, and will be resentful.

Neekaunissidoog! N'dawaemaudoog! For generations our forefathers freely ranged this land, lighting their fires where they wished and burying their dead in places now sacred. During our lives we, too, have enjoyed the land and its freedoms – and our children and their children should have the same rights. What I wish for you and for our children is a place where we can abide in peace and without want, where we can watch our children grow and hear them laugh, where we can smoke the pipe of friendship in our old age, and where we can die together and be buried near our ancestors ....

Neekaunissidoog! N'dawaemaudoog! You have my thoughts. That is all I wish to say.

DELIBERATIONS

There was a heavy silence after Mishi-Waub-Kaikaik sat down. Not only were his fellow chiefs deferent to each other's opinions, but they guarded their individual integrity. Moreover, the matter they had to discuss was both unfamiliar and weighty. Only after a long delay did the next speaker in the circle of chiefs and councillors rise to respond.

For three days the chiefs sat in council, looking into the question from different angles. There was no debate. Instead, the speakers sought illumination through mutual inquiry. Spokesmen prefaced their words with remarks like: "I have yet another understanding ...." And new interpretations were acknowledged with words such as: "Our brother has provided us with an idea ..." or "The Great Spirit has given me to understand...."

Nevertheless, at the end of their council the speakers were no closer to an agreement upon the answer they should give the White Man than they had been when they began their deliberations. Those who agreed to the surrender of land did so out of compassion for the poor, or in the belief that there was land enough to provide for all. Those who opposed the sale did so because of general distrust, and because there were no concrete details to discuss.

One by one, family by family, band by band, the visitors left the council. All promised to give the matter further consideration before the fall, when they would be summoned to treat with the White Man.

THE SECOND PROPOSAL

In early autumn, the officer returned to Ningiziwaush's village, accompanied again by soldiers and by an interpreter. He bore with him an urgent request from the Great White Father that the chiefs of all the tribes involved in the proposed treaty should assemble for a conference. For the second time, Ningi-

171

ziwaush sent his courier to relay the message and to invite nis
fellow chiefs to the conference – but on this occasion, not all
the chiefs arrived. Mizaun did not come; and neither did Mishi-Waub-Kaikaik. Like Ningiziwaush, both of these chiefs
were strongly against the selling of the land.

On the day of the conference, the officer, his captain, and
the interpreter assembled around a portable table set in front
of the officer's tent. The soldiers, all of them in full and
gleaming uniform, were there as well. When Ningiziwaush
was ready, he led his fellow chiefs towards the tent. The
chiefs – clad in plumes, fine buckskin, and chest shields of
bone adorned with shell – were also in full ceremonial dress.

Some twenty paces or so from the table, the tribal delegation stopped, and Ningiziwaush, accompanied only by his
courier, went forward. The officer rose from his chair behind
the table and moved to stand in front of it, an aide on his
right, and the interpreter on his left. Formally, he relayed the
greeting of the Great White Father to Ningiziwaush, and after
he had spoken, the interpreter translated his words.

Ningiziwaush listened to the friendly greeting, and then
replied. "Brother!" he said. "The Great Spirit has given us a
good day. We have thought about your proposal. But before we
can give you a final answer we need to understand the details
which we have not yet been shown."

The interpreter translated the chief's remarks, and the officer nodded. He extended his hand to Ningiziwaush, and the
two men shook hands. Sitting down again in his chair, the
officer watched while the chiefs sat in a semi-circle about the
table, where the aide was opening a document. Then, picking
up the document, the officer began to read. As the interpreter
translated as best he could, the chiefs listened carefully.

*... In consideration for the surrender of land, the Great
White Father will receive the tribe into his protection and
friendship, and the said tribe will agree to consider itself
under the protection of the Great White Father and no other
power whatsoever ...*

*... The party of the First Part will cause to be constructed
sixty good and substantial dwellings ...*

... The party of the First Part shall deliver without cost to the party of the Second Part wheat, corn, potatoes, and vegetables for cultivation for a period of five years ...

... The party of the First Part shall provide assistance in surveying the land to be retained by the tribe and subdividing it into twenty-five acre parcels ...

... The party of the First Part shall provide without cost such tools and implements as are necessary for cultivation...

... The party of the First Part shall pay or cause to be paid the sum of five thousand dollars to the chiefs and their families towards the benefit of the tribe ...

... The party of the First Part shall indemnify each member of the tribe and their descendants with the sum of one hundred dollars to be paid annually and in perpetuity ...

The reading – and the promises – went on for a long time.

Following the reading of the terms of the treaty, events moved quickly. The officer asked Ningiziwaush whether he and his fellow chiefs had understood the proposal, and if they were now willing to sign the document. The Indians had understood – but Ningiziwaush explained that they wished to hold private council in order to discuss some aspects of the treaty. Afterwards, went on Ningiziwaush, they would like to ask questions. Smiling in agreement, the officer watched as the chiefs withdrew.

Only two hours went by before the Indian delegation returned. The chiefs, said Ningiziwaush, had one important question to ask: Would they be permitted to hunt and to gather food on all the surrendered lands as they had done in the past? Again, the officer smiled. The answer, he said, was yes. And looking at the other chiefs behind Ningiziwaush, the officer reminded them of the additional promises in the treaty: promises for the provision of cattle and domestic animals for the start of farms; promises for the building of homes and the construction of schools and the arrival of teachers. All these things, the officer told them, would be theirs ....

Were they willing, now, to sign the treaty?

THE DECISION

Yes, decided the chiefs. It sounded fair and reasonable. They would sign the treaty. Only Ningiziwaush refused. He could not give his agreement unless the signing were unanimous – unless Mizaun and Mishi-Waub-Kaikaik were also present to agree to the terms of the proposal. Leaving the conference, Ningiziwaush remembered the words of Mishi-Waub-Kaikaik, his belief that no man had the right to give away the gift of the Great Spirit.

When Ningiziwaush had gone, the chiefs signed the treaty. Marking the document with an "X," each drew an image of his totem next to his mark. Afterwards, the officer offered them medals and beads, guns and powder, knives and axes and trinkets – gifts for those who signed the treaty. As a token of friendship and peace, the chiefs lit and smoked the sacred pipe. In exchange, and as a gesture of goodwill, the officer opened a keg of rum.

Before sunset, the chiefs and the officer signed yet another document. It was, smiled the officer, a duplicate of the original.

AFTERMATH

The following spring the soldiers returned to Ningiziwaush's village and drove the chief and his tribe from their homes. Throughout the summer the army pursued the fleeing group of ninety men, women, and children; and by the time another autumn had arrived, they had killed half of the band. Finally, Ningiziwaush gave himself up. He was taken away by the soldiers and never seen again.

As for those who had signed the treaty – they got homes in barren areas and cattle that were unfit. They received seed for infertile ground, and tools and implements without the forges to repair them. They acquired agents who cheated them and missionaries who banished their ceremonies; and they hunted and fished in territories that diminished under regulations that grew. They were given money – but not the amounts promised, and not in perpetuity. The beloved treaties they held were redrawn, revoked, voided, and repudiated.

174

Not immediately did the settlers come. But when they arrived, signatories and non-signatories of the treaties suffered alike. It made no difference.

The old, forgotten warning had proven to be true: *Your turn will come! You will lose your homes! You, too, will be wanderers!*

Appendices:
Original Ojibway Texts

PETITION TO THE NORTH (PAGE 109)

Keenwauh ayaubeetumaek keewaetinoong inaenimishinaung nongom geezhiguk tchi mino-bawaudjigaeyaung. Nauskau-wishinaung, abi-izhaumishinaung nongom tibikuk aen-dasso tibikuk gayae; abi gautawaendumook aen-dauyaung abi-mooshkinaeshiwik n'cheechaukinaunin tchi kezhaendu-maung w'onishishing. Waubundushinaung gayukawaudizin tchi kikaendumaung gae izhi gayaekaudiziyaung.

Zhaugodjitumowishinaung mayaunauduk tchi bawaudi-ziwaung. Kego inaenimishkaungaen tchi bawaudimaungibun zaugiziwin, kemauh maunaudaendjigaewin, kemauh wiyaez-hingaewin, kemauh naneenawaendumowin, tchi boduginí-kiyaungibun maunaudaendumowin.

Ganawaenimishinaung neebautibik maegwauh maemidi-gae gaugaetauwizissiwaung. Tibishko keewaetin aezhi mush-kowaunimuk zhaugoodinumowishinaung mayaunauduk; ti-bishko goon aezhi-pidugoonuyung aki ganawaenimishin-aung aen-datchiyaung. Kego gayae waebinushkaungaen; paumauh w'gee aubizeeshinaung, neenawind tibinawae tchi naunaugatawaendiziyaung.

PETITION TO THE WEST (PAGE 109)

Keenwauh ayaubeetumaek aepingishimook maumawissitu-mowishinaung mino-dae/aewin. Kikinowaezhowishinaung aenimook gayaekowaudizimeekunnuh tchi bwauh binooku-meewaungaen kemauh tchi bwauh winishinoowaungaen. Mino-inaenimishinaung tchi mino-dodomaung. Aussikowi-shin-aung washamae tchi zhawaenimungidawauh needji-bemaudizeenaunik, tchi zoongidae/aeyaung; tchi moozhiga-endaugoziyaung, tchi-nebawaukauyaung, tchi-zheebaendum-

179

aung; tchi gawaek dodowungit needjibemaudizeenaun; Inaenimishinaung tchi nissitowaubundumaung mayaunauduk,
n'onishishing gayae.

Kego inaenimishkaungaen tchi maunaudaenimungit n'eekaunissinaun kemauh n'dowaemaunaun; tchi augonaetizi-
waung n'mishomissinaubuneek w'kikinomauginiwiniwauh;
tchi daessidowaendumaung k'd'megoshaewinaunind tchi
gizhauwaessimaungidibun needji-bemaudizeenaunik, tchi
nissuyaendimaungiban n'd'waussaeyaubinduminaunin, kemauh tchi zhaugo-dae/aessiwaungibun.

Nindowaeto dush mino-dae/aewin. Inaenimishinaung tchi
manaudji/ungit Kitchi-Manitou, K'mishomissinaubuneek
k'okomissinaubuneek, k'kittisseeminaunik, w'gauh nibopu-
neek, zoongidae/aeshkowishinaung apee neenawaendu-
maung: mushkowaendumowishinaung chibwauh binookum-
mee/aung apee naneezaunaendaugook, tchi mino-neewigizi-
yaung; tchi aubawaewaenimungit n'eekaunissinaun, n'dowaemaunaun, gayae tchi dodumaung gauh izhi waussae-
yaubundumaung.

PETITION TO THE SOUTH (PAGE 110)

Kitchi-Manitou k'gee inaenimikonaun geegitowin tchi mino-i-
naendi/ing, tchi manaudji/ung k'manitouminaun. Onishi-
shin manitouwun gayae. Kitchitwauwaendaugoot.

Mezheg dush k'gee migooshkaussitaugozimim, kemauh
k'gee winigeekimaunaun k'weedjibimaundizeenaunik. Mezheg zaum weebah kemauh zaum weekauh k'geekimaunaun
k'weedjibimaudizeenaunik. Mezheg k'noondaewaudjimo-
mim, kemauh k'zaumaudjimomim. Mezheg k'gee matchi-
dazhimaunaun k'weedjibimaudizeenaun.

Keeshpin gageebaussitaugozi/ing k'gah gageebaudaeni-
mikomim, keeshpin gageeniwishkaudjimoying, kaween k'gah
daebawaetaugoosseemim.

Keeshpin dush wee mino-inaenimikoying, wee daebawae-
taukoying k'gah dodaumim gauh izhi-geekimikoyung kae-
tizdjig, tchi bizindumung chibwauh geegitoying, tchi mino-
taukoying auzhimino-inaunimuk zhawunonodin.

Apee kishkossiyaung gigishaeb n'd'aubizeeshinomim wee anookeeyaung. Maegwauh mozhigaendumaung n'mukwaenimaunaunik n'neekaunissinaunik, n'dawaemaunaunik gayae ayaunawitoodjik. K'weedjeehauwikonaun, gaegeebeengawaet, maumaundjigozit, gauwizidjik, zheegauquae, gaegeebinukawaet, wauh nindobawaudjigaet.

N'manitouminaun! N'zhawaenimaunaun n'neekaunissinaunik, n'dawaemaunaunik; n'gah mino-nawae/auninik nongom geezhiguk aezhi-kishki/aeyiziyaung. N'gah kikinowinowaumim gaegeebeengawaet, n'gah aunkae-omaumim maemaundjigozit, n'gah koginaumim gauwizidjig, n'gah gautawaenimaumim zheegauquae, n'gah gaganoodumowaumim gaegeebinukawaet, n'gah aussikouwaumim wauh nindobawaudjigaet.

Inaendun tchi mizheenowaut gauwissaungunuk, tchi mizheenowaut mandauminuk, tchi omishishing n'mushkikeeminaun.

Manitouwit Teemigameeng
Manitouwit Pishu-geeshkibik
Manitouwit Tibikutinik
Manitouwit Naunibomowin
Manitoushkung zugussikodaetchigaewin.
Kego!
Bebaumaenimishkaungaen
Nebau/aung
Naunaugatawaendumaung
Apaenimohaung
Manitoukae/aung.
Inaenim n'cheejaukinaun
Tchi neebitaushkauwaut
Mindjindim auzhook mindjindim
Miziwae auyaukawaukummigauk
N'inaendumowinauning
Mishowigeezhigoong
Wee dittumowaut
Bizaun-dae/aewin.

APPENDIX B – PETITIONS OF THE WAUBUNOWIN

PETITION TO THE NORTH (PAGE 119)

Keenwauh ayaubeetumaek keewaetinoong k'maumauyauwi-mikoom, k'manaudjikoom gayae. Aegautchitook k'nodiniwiniwaun, zaegakautchitumook tchi kitchi-beboozinook kemauh tchi zaumaugonugaupun ondjih tchi waubunishkauyaung kakinah aenditchiyaung; tchi aukozissigoowaupun n'needjaunissinaunik; zaum tchi kitimaugitowaupun n'mishomissinaunik n'okomissinaunik gayae. K'abi naussikaugoom dush tchi geekimiyaung. Naudimooshishinaung tchi zoongiziyaung tchi zheebaendumaung gayae tchi waubunishkauyaung. Weedookowishinaung tchi mukowaendumaung keeshpin mino-inaukinigaessiwaung, kemauh wi-inaendumaung keeyaubih wee abiwaubung wee abi-kikinooniwung gayae, n'gah inigauhaumim keeyaubih w'wauh abi indaudizidjik.

Mukwaenimishinaung dush, daessido-aenimishinaung gayae apee abi-gagawaedabaenimiyaung; apee abi binaukawaebinudowauh metigook; apee abi koonauzhiwaegowauh geegoohnuk; apee abi aumowaegowauh n'suhyaehnaunik. Zhawaenimik moozo, wauhwaushkaesh, mukwoh, amik, adjidimoh. Gautawaenimik tchi ganaundiziwaut; w'dowiziwuk gayae weenwauh tchi bimaudiziwaut.

Kego zaum gaesikah kemauh zaum weebah abi-digooshinookaegoon; Kego weesikitgokaegoon, kego zaum ganawaesh abi daneekaegoon.

Zhawaenimik gayae maubah ae-yaukozit. Inaenimik tchi zhauboweet, tchi ganaundizoot meenwauh ningoting.

PETITION TO THE SOUTH (PAGE 119)

Keenwauh ayaubeetumaek zhawunoong k'maumiyauwimikoom, k'manaudjikoom gayae. Keeshpin nongoom neebin

gauh bimisaekimiguk gee mino-weesiniyaung, missiwae gee
neebitaushkauyaung, gee waubumimungowauh n'neekaunissinaunik, n'dowaemaunaunik gayae, gee waubundumaung
aenaussikummigauk, aenkummigaut Mizukummik'quae,
n'gee mino-shaemim gayae: keeshpin gayae neebunuh ma-
shki-aki gee zugukunumaung, neebunuh weeyauss, geegohn,
mandamin gee maunwindoonimaung, keenwauh tibinawae
ondjih; keeshpin gayae pakadaessiwaung nongoom bebong,
kemauh missugawaudizissiwaung keenwauh k'd'indowino-
wauh.

K'begossaenimikoom dush tchi kikino-waezhiwiyaung.
K'gauh izhi minododowaungibunaenuk n'neekaunissinaunik,
n'dowaemaunaunik gayae. Inaeninimishinaung tchi nau-
naugatawaenimungit w'oshkineegidjik, kaetizidjik gayae:
w'gauh maudjaupuneek, gayae: w'gae-ganaundizidjik, w'ae-
yaukozidjik gaye. Naussaub gauh izhi-shumiyaung mee
naussaub gae izhi-gautawaenimungowauh ae-neenimizidjik,
ae-maumaundjigozidjik, ae-yaukozidjik, ae-zheegau/odjik;
gawizidjik gayae. Mukowaumishinaung tchi zoongdae/ae-
nyaung, tchi zheebaendumaung gayae.

Zhawaenimishinaung, kego inaenimishikaungaen tchi
wi-inaendumaung. Tibishko aezhi aubowishkowaek Mizukummik'quae; aubowishkowishinaung tchi mino-dittumaung
aezhi-mino inaukinigaeyaung; naussaub meenkaunaehnse
aezhi ani-mandauminiwit. Keeshpin bino-kummeeyaung, au-
bowaewaenimishinaung.

Zhawaenimik gayae n'dowaemaunaun, Naundiwi/ik aesh-
kum tchi ani-boniweesigitoot tibishko aezhi ningiziwaek goon,
aezhi geezhogimitoyaek gumeen. Maeno inaenimik tchi aubi-
zeeshing, tchi neebinishinoot tchi oshishaehnit keeyaubih
dassing.

Kego zaum ganawaesh indaendikaegon; kego winaeni-
mishkaungaen minik aepeetaendiyaek weebah abi-neebini-
shawishkaung.

PETITION TO THE EAST (PAGE 120)

Keenwauh ayaubeetumaek waubunong, k'maumiyauwimikoom, k'manaudjikoom gayae. Abi waussaeshkumaek n'd'a-
keeminaun, kakinah gaego k'abi aubizeeshkaunauwauh:

183

w'gauh nebaumiguk. K'd'aubizeeshkawauwauk binaessiwuk gae ningumtaugayaek k'd'aubizeeshkaunauwaun wausko-naehn gae shpooshkaugin; k'd'aubizeeshkawauwauk adjiki-mook goonkisaehnsuk gae duminoodjik; k'd'aubizeeshkawi-mim tchi bumeekumaung waegidowgwaen anookeewin gae digooshinoomigudogwaen; k'd'aubizeeshkawauwauk n'need-jaunissinaunik washamae tchi kishkiyaewiziwaut wee mino-dodumowaut. K'waussaeyaushkaunauwauh aki gauh psho-geeshkaumiguk; k'gee zaugidjininiwaezhiwim aundi gauh danee/aung aupitanebowinaung.

Aezhi waussaeshkumaek aki, apaegish gayae neenawind izhi geekimungit n'needjaunissinaunik tchi maumenowau-bundumowaut. Inaenimishinaung tchi aunkaenimungdo-wauh kikaendumowin n'mishomissinaubuneek, n'okomissi-naubunee gauh aunkaenimauki/aungibun, tchi nibwaukau-waut, tchi zhawaendjigaewaut tchi zoongidae/aewaut, tchi kishki/aewiziwaut gayae, Inaenim tchi waussaeyaubindu-mowaut, tchi minododumowaut gayae.

Kego inaenimishkaungaen tchi wi-inaenimungit n'need-jaunissinaunik maegwauh daebugwaendumaung. N'd'apae-nimikoognaun tchi gayaek inaukinikae/aung, aezhi apaeni-mungidowauh. Mee aezhi-pagidinumiwungit. Apaegish mino-daupinumowaut, koginauwitowaut.

Zhawaenimik gayae n'dowaemaunaun. Tibishko gauh izhi aubizeeshimishinaung, aubizeeshimik. Keeyaubih w'dah mi-no-dodum.

Inaenimishinaung tchi mino-dittumaung nongom geezhi-guk, waubung, minik gayae keeyaubi gae abi waubunong-waen.

PETITION TO THE WEST (PAGE 121)

Keenwauh ayaubeetumaek aephingishimook k'maumiyau-wimikoom, k'manaudjikoom gayae. Aendassoh geezhiguk k'mukwaewaendumimim n'bimaudiziwininaun; beedaubung, oshkibimaudiziwin: ani-pingishimook, kaetae/audiziwin; ae-peetissaet geeziss, aepeetissaemiguk bimaudiziwin, Mino-waunigwaendaugut waubunduming abi-waubung; ani-pingi-shimook. Waegwaen kaetizigwaen kitch-meenikowizih. K'mu-kwaewaendumowimim wauh izhiwaebiziyaung aubiding.

184

Ani-pingishing geezis, aezhi-gazheeaussigaet chibwauh nakaewae/aussigaet n'kikaendaumim boonaussigaet: naussaub n'kikaendaumim tch-abi-waubung meenwauh, kauween tibishko k'bimaudiziwinaunin. Binaessiwuk kikaendaunauwauh ani-pingishimook mee wae-ondji aeni-naneewitaugoziwaut; wauwauskoonaehn wae-ondji shpushkaumiguk; adjikimoohnsuk, goonkissaehnsuk wae-ondji zheemeewaut: Neenawind, ayaekozi/aung n'gah awoh gawishimomim. Missowauh gae izhipegossaendumowaungobun tchi bonigeezhigussinook, tchi shkwauh-bimaudizissiwaung, potch w'dah boonaussigae geezis, k'gah nebomim. Tibishko aezhi tibikaubiminaugook, mee naussaub gae izhi-neenimizit baemaudizit beenish tchi nebot tchi ani-digooshing woodih waukweeng aen-dazhi-daneenit w'kitisseemun w'mishomissun, n'okomissun gayae. Aezhi gazhee/aussigaet geezis chibwauh tibikuk mee aezhi pegossaendumaung tchi minowaubuminaugook n'dodumowininaun tchi nawautchitowaut n'needjaunissinaunik. Apaegish aezhi waussaeyaussigaet geezis w'dah kikiniwauzinauzinaugozinoon d'dodumowinaunin; apaegish gayae tchi mino-dae/aeyaung apee maudjauyaung, digooshinaung waukweeng.

Zhawaenimik gayae n'dowaemaunaun. Gautawaenimik nongom tibikuk, tchi waubundung gayae ween meenwauh waubuninik; tchi kotugitoosik apee kishkozit.

Inaenimishinaung tchi mino-nebauyaung; tchi mino-bawaudjigaeyaung; inaenimishinaung tchi dodumaung aezhiwaussaeyaubundumaung. Tchi daebawaeyaung, tchi daebawaetaugoyaung, n'dah izhi-pegossaendaumim.

(PAGES 160-161)

Kitchi-Manitouminaun, k'manaudjiko. K'gee Kitchi-zhawae-nimimim. K'gee inaenimimim tchi bemaudiziyaung meen-wauh tchi waubundiyaung neezho-beboon gauh ikowaubun-diyaungibun. K'gee koginauh wauwaushkaesh, amik, addi-kameg, benaessi gayae, nomgom w'gauh pagidinuhmaugi-yungit w'bemaudiziwininauh keenawind tchi weesinihing. K'gee inaendum gayae tchi mino-geezhiguk ae-apeetchi zu-guswaediyaung. K'gee wizhitoon aki aendi-daneeyaung; aen-dazhi dabaendaugoziyaung.

Mizukummukiquae n'd'izhi-manaudji/aumim. Akeeng n'dabaendaugozimim. Nongom dush n'wee debaukinaumim w'gauh izhi-begossaenimikoyaung aendogwaen aeinaendau-goziwaungaen tchi aunkaenimaung awih daebaendiziwaung. Kauween n'gawaekiwaendizeemin aendowgwaen inaendau-goziwaungen tchi meegwaeyaung awih w'gauh meenikoya-ung, tibishko gae izhi meegwaewaugaen bakeeskowaugun, pawaugun, kemauh metigwaub. Waussaeyaubundumowi-shinaung dush tchi gawaek-inaukinigaeyaung.

Keenwauh ayaubeetumaek keewaetinoong inaenimishi-naung neegaun tchi kikinowautchiwaubungaeyaung non-gom zuguswaediyaung. Naussaub waesseehnuk aezhi ki-kaendumowaut abi-bebooninik, aezhi kikaendumowaut benaessiwuk abi-bigumuk mee-dush augwoonaeshinoowaut, inaenimishinaung naussaub tchi waubundumaung neegaun wauh izhiwaebuk tchi wizheetauyaung. N'geewidaendau-mim, mee dush w'ondjih maumowih zuguswaediyaung wa-shamae tchi nissitotomaung. K'dah begossaenimiko dush tchi inaenimiyaung tchi waubi/aung aushiwaewijewinaung, ae-numook meekun, wauh izhi-waebutogwaen ani-waubung. Baukaukinimowishinaung, n'shkeehnzhigoonaun, n'tuwugunaun, n'd'inaendumowininaun gayae. Keeshpin wee mino-dodowungit n'weedji-bemaudizeenaun nongom; n'needjaunissinaun gayae, aubidaek, n'gah gawaekaendaumim gae izhi matchi-dodomaungibun kemauh gae izhi mino-dodomaungibun aen-inaukinigaeyaung nongom. Keeshpin gayae neegaun-waubundumaung wauh izhiwaebuk, kemauh n'dauh gawaek-inaukinigaemin washamae tchi waenipuniziwaut baemaudizidjik, kauween dush tchi zunugizissigowauh.

Keenwauh ayaubeetumaek aepingishimook inaenimishinaung tchi nissitotowaendumaung nongom maundah (awih) wauh nindo-daebagwaendumaung. N'mauwindjidimim, dush tchi maumowissitooyaung n'd'inaendumowininaun, n'dae/inaun nawutch tchi gawaek-inaendumaung gae inaukinegaewaungibunaen kemauh gae inaukinigaessowaungibunaen. K'd'begossaenimikoom dush nongom tchi geekimi/aung, tchi gagauzoongimi/aung, tchi auskohi/aung maegwauh zuguswaedi/aung; w'dah abi baezhigoomigut dush n'd'inaendumowininaun, n'debaukinigaewininaun. Keenwah, zhigoh gauh neebitaushkumaek meekunnuh, weendumowishinaung ae-numook tchi binuhkummeessowaung.

Keenwauh ayaubeetumaek zhauwunoong inaenimishinaung tchi gawaek-inaukinigaeying. Kauween weekauh awiyah w'gee nakawaeshkizeenaudook; w'gee nawautchitoosseenaudook maundah nongom wauh dibaudindumung, wauh dibaubeeshkoodoo/ing. Kauween gaego dagoomigussinoon k'bemaudziwiwinauning gae kikinowautchitoo/ingobun; kauween gaego dagoomigussinoon k'daebawaewendumowininaung gae naussaubissidoo/ingobun maundah nongom wauh dibaukinuhmung. K'wauweendumaugoomim tchi mino-doduminung. Apaegish gaegaet daebawaetumungibun. Auneehn dush gae izhi gawaek-inaendumaungibun. Auneehn gae izhi gawaek-dibaukinuhmaungibun? Miziwae innuhmidoon meekunnun; Mizheenidoon baebikaun inaukinigaewinun. Aunind onishishinoon; aunind maunaudidoon. Keeshpin wee binukummeesiyaung, keeshpin wee gawaek-inaugudooyaung meekunnuh, inaendaugoot tchi nissitotowaubundumaung wauh ani-izhauyaung; tchi nissitotowaubundumaung iniw ae-numookin kitimaugoziwinning iniw/gayae ae-gawaek-imookin. Zunugut bemaudiziwin.

Kauween n'd'inaenduzeemim tchi wani-inaukinigaeyaung tchi inigau/iyungit n'weedji-bemaudizeenaunik, n'needjaunissinaunik gayae; weenwauh gae bimoondumowaut keeshpin mauzh-inaukinigaeying. K'd'begossaenikoom dush tchi aungawaumaenimiyaung, tchi gagauzoongaenimiyaunggayae nongom tchi gawaek-inaukinigaeyaung tchi mino-dodowungdowauh awih dush n'weedji-bemaudizeenaunik, n'needjaunissinaunik gayae.

Keenwauh ayaubeetumaek waubunoong inaenimishinaung tchi mushko-inaendumaung, tchi mushko-dae/aeyaung gayae tchi dodomaung ae-inaukinigaeyaung. N'gah daebawaewaendaugozimim dush. Aubiding geezhau-inaukingaeng, kemauh daebindowaeng, kauween inaendaugozinoon tchi izhaetaugibun, kemauh tchi augoonaetauginbun. N'goosikeewaudaendaumim, n'zaegaendaumim aubidaek n'gah zhaugoodaendaumim waegidogwaen ae-zaegaendumowaungaen. Keeshpin inaenimugwaung baekaunizidjik n'd'akeeminaun, inaeninimishinaung tchi manaudjito/yaung aezhidaebindoyaung; kemauh, inaenimishinaung tchi mushkowaendumaung keeshpin augoonaetumaung. Zoongidae/aeshkawishinaung.